Testimo

"As a fellow sufferer from addiction and shame-based mental illness, I can't stress enough how much it has meant to me to discover this insightful book. Debra Whittam casts an unashamed light on her shame-based childhood and subsequent decent into a sea of addiction, loneliness and denial. I was skeptical when I first picked up the book as there have been a great many books about these subjects. After reading it, my spirit has a renewed hope in turning my own shame-based afflictions into a truly peaceful existence."

—JULIE MASON,
Legal & Organizational Leadership Professional

"Am I Going To Be Okay? is an enormously helpful book. Debra Whittam weaves her personal experiences with those of her clients into a thought-provoking book that touches profoundly on the relationship between family fears and frustrations and how they affect our levels of self-esteem. The result is a story that will be helpful to all who might need to throw off fear and frustration and gain the courage and self-confidence to greet each new day"

—DR. CASEY MCNEAL,
Author, *Building Relationships:
Effective Strategies for How to Work With People*

"This is a powerful book. I hear so much of my own self-doubt in her words, so much of not just "will I be okay?" but, is it even possible for someone like me to ever be okay? It took great courage for her to write this book. It will definitely change lives."

—REV. CHARLOTTE FOUST,
Community Spiritual Center

Am I Going To Be Okay?

Weathering the Storms
of
Mental Illness, Addiction, and Grief

BY DEBRA WHITTAM

Editor: Judi Moreo
Cover Art: Jeff Tift
Typesetting: Ambush Graphics

Library of Congress Control Number: 2015955245
ISBN: 978-0-99668817-0-8
1. Memoir 2. Women-Psychology 3. Psychology - Applied

Disclaimer
This book includes the author's personal accounts of dealing with mental illness, addiction, and grief as well as others' true stories. All personal stories that appear in this book have been used with permission. In some cases, names, dates, and circumstances have been changed to protect anonymity, but many individuals have requested that their real names be used.

This book is for educational purposes. It is not intended to replace medical advice. This publication is intended to provide authoritative and accurate information, and it is up-todate and timely as of its date of publication; however, it is not meant to replace the services of a trained professional, physician, support group or recovery group.

This book is sold with the understanding that the publisher and author are not rendering individual psychological or medical services of any kind to the reader. Should such services be necessary, please consult an appropriate professional.

Turning Point International, Inc.
1452 W. Horizon Ridge Parkway, Henderson, Nevada 89012

{ ☂ }

Dedicated to
"the little girl who no one wanted"
my mom
Judy Mastroianni Neadle

EPIGRAPH

"When I was little, I agreed and they were right.
Then in middle school, I didn't agree
but figured they must be right.
By the time I was in high school,
I realized I didn't agree,
They were not right, but I couldn't say anything."

—DEBRA WHITTAM

Contents

Forward.. xi

Preface.. xiii

Acknowledgments... xvi

Cast of Characters.. xviii

Chapter 1:   The Driving Lesson 21

Chapter 2:   When the Doctor Called.................................... 29

Chapter 3:   The Beginnings of Wanderlust 37

Chapter 4:   The Neadle Farm 43

Chapter 5:   The Lost Neadle... 47

Chapter 6:   Where Abandonment Came From 55

Chapter 7:   Surviving Aunt Rose 63

Chapter 8:   In and Out of Church 69

Chapter 9:   Things We Never Talk About 73

Chapter 10: Frightened and Barely Holding On 85

Chapter 11: Real Life Dramas... 93

Chapter 12: Wanting To Be That Girl 99

Chapter 13: My New York State of Mind 107

Chapter 14: Chasing Love and Choosing Poorly 115

Chapter 15: Wife, Mother, and Teetering on the Brink....... 121

Chapter 16: The World Comes Unglued 129

CONTENTS CONTINUED NEXT PAGE

Chapter 17: Facing the Truth 135

Chapter 18: Resisting The Curriculum 145

Chapter 19: Having the Talk 151

Chapter 20: Dealing With The Hard Stuff................................. 163

Chapter 21: Have They All Gone Crazy?................................... 171

Chapter 22: The Tough Job of Making Changes 179

Chapter 23: Longing For Words I Never Heard......................... 185

Chapter 24: Leaving The Sofa 193

Chapter 25: Making It Okay To Let Go 203

Chapter 26: Our Hospice Angel 211

Chapter 27: Where Is She Really?.. 219

Chapter 28: Through The Eyes of Others................................. 223

Chapter 29: Mom's Legacy.. 229

Epilogue 235

Appendix 239

Photographs 245

Bibliography 250

About the Author 251

Forward

THIS IS A POWERFUL BOOK AND A VERY PERSONAL ONE. DEBRA Whittam is one brave lady to be willing to share her journey from her dysfunctional childhood through alcoholism to health and wholeness. She tells her story well – and her words trigger feelings that go with our own stories, even though they may be very different stories.

Debra is an experienced, triumphant adult who is willing to divulge her innermost secrets. She has struggled, worked, and persevered. She has learned how to make things happen for herself. She has shared her knowledge and many valuable lessons acquired on her personal road to success. Stories help us see and understand that other people have gone through similar experiences to ours. Experience is a wise teacher…whether it is our own or someone else's.

This book encourages each of us to have a better, more meaningful life. It shows us how one woman reclaimed her power. If you put to use the knowledge, guidance, and inspiration she offers, I am confident you will come to recognize the success story that lies within you.

—JUDI MOREO,
Author, *You Are More Than Enough:
Every Woman's Guide to Purpose, Passion, and Power*

Preface

IN MY THERAPIST'S OFFICE, DURING MY FIRST YEAR OF RECOVERY from alcoholism, I saw one of her graduate school psychology books on her bookshelf. It was sitting alongside many of her self-help books which I had borrowed during the past year. I read several hoping to find a cure from my irrepressible anxiety that I had previously drunk away. I imagined the wordy text was far from my ability to comprehend as I was at that time only able to retain small bits of information. I asked my therapist if I could borrow that college text titled "Human Growth and Development." I read it from cover to cover within a short amount of time and, surprisingly, was able to digest and retain it. I had to quit doubting my ability. Being hard on myself was no longer the answer. I wanted more.

That following summer I enrolled in a graduate course of the same name. I wanted to see if I could retain enough material to pass a higher level learning class. I loved it and I got an A.

No longer living in a world governed by my need to numb myself through copious amounts of alcohol, I started doing what I wanted to do with my life. Encountering the self-doubt I had always carried within me became the guidepost by which I continued to prove my "what ifs" unnecessary in order to keep myself safe.

My intention in writing this book is to reach out to all who suffer and struggle with being frozen in fear of "what if." This book may trigger emotions that have been shoved down so far they might not have a clear story to them yet. It might trigger memories of resentments, regrets or painful unhealed episodes of your life. These moments may have happened long, long ago or may have been more recent. We go back into the past to find answers. The idea is not to stay there long, but to find healing through understanding the 'why' of it. Then begin our process of learning to self-sooth and love ourselves. Nothing is going to happen that you can't handle. Nothing.

Isolated within my world of fear, I wouldn't attempt anything outside of that small world. I had no foundation to stand on as a springboard toward finding out who I really was, so I joined a 12-Step group. The beauty of being in a community of recovery, from whatever we might be working on, brings connection. That is what I needed so badly.

I hope, within these pages, you are able to find a spark that ignites your longing for more. I urge you to find your own path of being okay by whatever non-mood altering way that makes sense to you; even, or especially, if it is unfamiliar to you. In writing this book, I intended to show how we can all go through our fears and do "it" anyway, whatever "it" is.

Letting go of fear suggests we "just breathe" and be ourselves. The "how" of being okay is within these pages and within yourself. Stop listening to the repeated echoes of old messages in your head, messages like "You've done it again," "You aren't good enough," "You should just give up." These messages cause you to doubt yourself. Instead, listen to the other voice inside which says, "You can do this,"

"There is a way." Don't ignore it. Don't push it away. Don't argue with it. That voice is there, even if you can't hear it and I am here to help you find it. I look forward to hearing you say, "I AM going to be okay."

—DEBRA WHITTAM, MSED., LPC, CT, CCADC, CCDPD

Acknowledgments

TO JILL, NATASHA AND VIRGINIA FOR GIVING OF THEMSELVES SO THAT I might live. Without the guidance from their experiences, and out of those experiences encouraged by their strength and hope came the courage to breathe, walk and talk one step at a time, one day at a time.

To my beloved siblings, Denise, Diana, David and Dina. Without them I would be even more selfish and self-centered.

To my beloved father, Richard Neadle. Your survival skills have served me well.

To Carol Henderson, author of *Losing Malcolm*, who encouraged me to keep writing through her amazing writing workshops and guidance through her own pain.

To Nick Keppler, writer for *The Village Voice*, who encouraged me to 'elaborate' in my early manuscript: to "show" through my writing, not tell.

To my beloved friend, Kathy Jo, with whom I had a lunch date that I had planned to cancel, but didn't. It was at that lunch that I was connected with my wonderful editor!

To my "Pleasers Group," Gail, Sue, Laura, Darlene, Torri and Melissa, who are no longer "pleasers" but honoring themselves by modeling what it looks like to live in the world without guilt or fear of not pleasing others. They show the way for others to do the same.

To Trudy, James and Frances who inspire me to not give up.

To all the participants in Carol Henderson's writing workshops in North Carolina and the participants in the writing workshop at the American University in Paris. To Eric Freez, leader of the Paris workshop and author of *Dominant Traits*, who encouraged me to keep writing and get a really good editor!

To all my wonderful cousins, who made a positive difference in my life.

To my former husband, Chet, with whom I have the most wonderful children.

To my children, Chet and Katherine, who are compassionate, independent people who have chosen their own paths in life with courage and conviction.

To Debra Myers, my yoga instructor and stress management guide. Your wise counsel of "just breathe" remains with me always.

I am indebted to my editor, Judi Moreo, who fell in love with my story and encouraged me until I believed her that it was worth telling, and to the members of her editing team, Judy Weaver, Joan S. Peck, and Charlotte Foust.

And to my mom, Judith Mastroianni Neadle, that little girl who no one wanted, know that I wanted you, desperately. I hope it made a difference.

Cast of Characters

My Father's Family

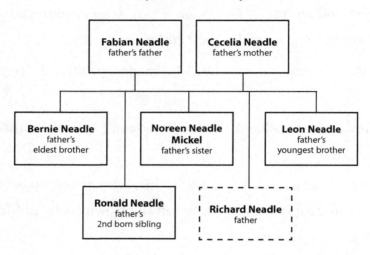

Fabian Neadle
father's father

Cecelia Neadle
father's mother

Bernie Neadle
father's
eldest brother

Noreen Neadle Mickel
father's sister

Leon Neadle
father's
youngest brother

Ronald Neadle
father's
2nd born sibling

Richard Neadle
father

My Mother's Family

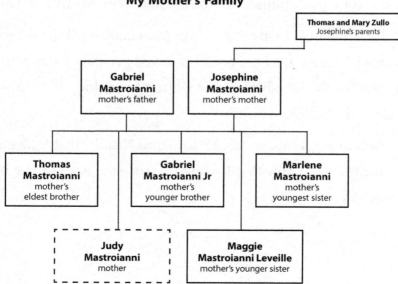

Thomas and Mary Zullo
Josephine's parents

Gabriel Mastroianni
mother's father

Josephine Mastroianni
mother's mother

Thomas Mastroianni
mother's
eldest brother

Gabriel Mastroianni Jr
mother's
younger brother

Marlene Mastroianni
mother's
youngest sister

Judy Mastroianni
mother

Maggie Mastroianni Leveille
mother's younger sister

My Mother's Immediate Family

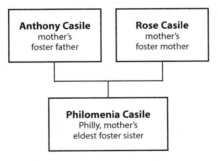

Richard Neadle
father

Judy Mastroianni
mother

Debbie Neadle Whittam
me

David Neadle
brother

Dina Neadle Hennessey
youngest sister

Adam Hennessey
(Dina's husband)

Chet Whittam 3rd
son

Katherine Whittam
daughter

TWINS

Denise Neadle Paska
sister, eldest of the twins by 4 minutes

Diana Neadle Kellogg
sister, youngest twin

Paul Paska
(Denise's husband)

John Kellogg
(Diana's husband)

My Mother's Foster Family

Anthony Casile
mother's foster father

Rose Casile
mother's foster mother

Philomenia Casile
Philly, mother's eldest foster sister

Others

Dave *(High school boyfriend)* • Geoff *(College boyfriend - New York City boyfriend)*
Chet Whittam Jr *(Ex-husband)* • Luisa Roney *(Nanny)*
Donna Harding *(Hospice nurse)* • Kathy *(Hospice nurse)*
Rob *(Funeral Home Director)*

CHAPTER ONE

The Driving Lesson

"AM I GOING TO BE OKAY?" IT WAS THE SUMMER BEFORE I STARTED kindergarten. I had just turned five that June and was sitting in the back seat of our neighbor's 1961 Buick listening as Gladys tried to teach Mom how to drive. Mom was crying and struggling with the stick shift attempting to drive down a long, lonely stretch of road aptly named Thousand Acre Road. We were about a mile from our house just outside of our village of Delanson, New York, but it seemed as though we were in the middle of nowhere. "Am I going to be okay?" It was the first time I remember hearing those words. It would not be the last.

Mom was 4' 11", weighed 105 lbs. and was petrified of being in that driver's seat. She needed to sit on two large phone books to see over the steering wheel and to reach the pedals even though the long, bench type front seat was pulled as far forward as possible. Gladys, who was a large German woman, was pressed up against the dashboard and now was more ornery than normal. Mom was begging Gladys to stop the driving lessons. She didn't want to do it anymore.

Gladys was a part-time nurse at Ellis Hospital in Schenectady and had very little patience. I can't imagine how she became the choice to teach Mom how to drive but here we were idling on this dirt road waiting for something to happen. Mom continued shaking and crying each time she stalled the car, trying unsuccessfully to get it into first gear. Gladys firmly commanded her to stop crying, let out the clutch, push on the gas, and "drive the goddamn car!" This only caused Mom to escalate into a higher level of panic. She looked over her shoulder at me with tear-filled eyes, pleading for help, "Debbie, am I going to be okay?"

"Yes, Mom," I said in the most reassuring voice my five-year-old self could come up with. "Isn't this fun?"

"Oh, for Christ sake, Judy," Gladys bellowed from the passenger side, "Let your foot off the clutch, push on the goddamn gas and drive!" She didn't want to remain in that car much longer either. I took in the tension of that scene, wanting to be as calm, clear-headed, and loving as I could be. I knew Gladys' harsh ways wouldn't work. Interestingly, most people Mom was surrounded by were like Gladys – Dad, my aunts and uncles, and friends – all impatient with her fears of everything.

"Mom, you are going to be okay," I encouraged her as I repeatedly jumped up from my seat and leaned over the long, hard ridge along the back of her seat. My stomach ached from balancing on it so I could show her the gears and pedals. There were no seat belts in those days so I was free to see and be a part of the drama unfolding before me.

Mom was in her early twenties when I was born. At this point, five years later, she realized if we waited for my father to drive us anywhere, like to the movies to see Disney's *Cinderella*, it wasn't going to happen. Dad had far more important things to do. He felt his time would be wasted doing something as silly as a movie. She and I were on our own to see the "magical world of Disney" or any of the rest of the world at all. She had never wanted to drive, ever. I remember thinking if I could drive at the age of five, it would've been fine with her. Mom's desire to get out of town for the 25-mile drive to Schenectady motivated her to overcome her anxieties, get off the sofa and learn to drive. We were both excited to plan a trip to "the city" for a movie at Proctors Theater with lunch at Carl's Department Store afterward. It was a very high society thing to do back then. Plus the thing that motivated Mom most was my aunts could all drive, and she wanted to keep up with what they were doing.

It was second nature for me, even that early on, to reassure her that everything was going to be okay. The reality was, with Mom at the wheel, we were not okay at all. I was sure from my perch balancing on my stomach that I had a far better view of the road than she did.

Mom was peaceful, calm and content only when she was lying on her right side on the left corner of the sofa. Any plans or action much more than that could cause her anxieties to rise dramatically, sometimes even bringing her to the point of blanking out.

It took every kind of fortitude for Mom to stay in the car and attempt again and again to make it move forward. Her anxieties were equal to a commander of a shuttle about to blast off. This car was way too much for Mom, and she wanted to be at home on her sofa.

Gladys had been our next-door neighbor for three years now, ever since we moved into the three bedroom ranch home my parents, grandparents, aunts and uncles worked hard to build in 1959. She had talked Mom off the ledge many times before this. Once, I got my finger stuck in the front screen door of our house. Mom screamed and ran to Gladys' house, leaving me stuck in the door. Left there to fend for myself, a pattern that followed throughout my life, I had a twinge of panic that she just might not come back. I jiggled the handle of the metal door and finally got my finger out by myself.

I was crying when Mom and Gladys found me sitting on the front porch sucking on my finger. I wasn't as upset about the pain of my smashed finger as I was scared and needed my Mom. As the two of them walked across the grass between our houses, there was no more panic in Mom's eyes. They were giggling and looked like there was some inside joke. Mom looked at me and said, "Oh, stop crying. You're fine."

She and Gladys went inside the house as I sat there on the cold cement, confused. That didn't seem very nice. I needed someone to tell ME that everything was going to be okay. I still wanted to be taken care of. It was ever so subtle but the message was clear. It was almost as though I had done something wrong. Shame and subtle ridicule was the sound of Mom's reassurance. Most problems I encountered in my young life, either physically or emotionally, were either because I had done something wrong, or there was something wrong with me. Those were the choices. Let the ridicule begin.

> Cheryl Huber, a Buddhist monk who has a monastery in Northern California, travels sharing experiences of how to meditate, and has written a wonderful, easy-to-read book aptly titled, "There is Nothing Wrong With You." In this book, she begins with a litany of assaults which many of us heard from our early years that remain with us, intruding on a daily basis, such as: "What is wrong with you? Didn't I just tell you not to do that? Don't look at me that way! Stop crying! You are so dumb! Why didn't you already know that? Who doesn't know this?" This speaks to our inner self-hate monitor which was at the beginning of that time that we can't really pinpoint and seems to have no end. It is the time when our self-image, our core beliefs, are planted, nurtured and bear fruit in our anxieties, addictions, and actions.

However, back on that day of the driving lesson, I took in every look on Mom's face as she struggled through the hell of those moments. Here she was trembling with fear behind the wheel of this monster moving vehicle and enduring being bellowed at by Gladys. "Can we just go home?" she asked. She was finished for the day!

From an early age, I was intensely aware of her every worry, every fear. It became a normal part of my life. I took in every look on Mom's face, every choking catch in her throat. I wanted to rescue her, help her, and make her fears go away. I wanted to make her happy. Years later, I had more of a love/hate relationship with that part of her, but at the time, her survival was my main concern.

I kept reassuring her, "Mom it's going to be okay – just let go of that pedal thing, push on that pedal over there and the stick thingy does an H. First, go up on the top – on that side of the H." I pointed to where she needed to have her hands and feet to make the car move and not stall. I had paid close attention to Dad when he tried to teach Mom to drive many times before. In Dad's car, Mom needed three phone books and chunks of wood taped to the pedals in order to see over the steering wheel. Dad wouldn't let her move the seat forward. He refused to be smashed up against the dashboard. My guess is Gladys took over those lessons when things with Dad didn't go so well. But, at least, I learned. He was my role model for everything, like being strong, courageous and powerful. I wanted to be just like him.

I watched how he did most everything and I still have many of his mannerisms and sayings today. "Shit or get off the pot" is one. It flows right off the tongue. So, in that car with Gladys, it was now my turn to help Mom…to be the one who saved her with kindness and patience. She paid attention to me when I did that.

"Yes, Mom, you are going to be okay." It was exhausting work to reassure her since these emotional upheavals happened often. I don't remember hearing her say those things back to me. But, she must have.

Finally, figuring there was no other way out of this mess, Mom shored up the courage from somewhere, managed to push on something right, and the car moved forward without stalling. I softly said, "Yea, Mom!" She turned to look at me, and her body relaxed just a little bit. I was relieved to see her less terrified. Mom was going to be okay, and I was, too.

Mom smiled with pride as she continued driving 20 miles an hour down the road. Then, Gladys said, "Jesus Christ, Judy, you need a five-year-old to get you to push the goddamn gas."

Mom did eventually learn how to drive and passed her driver's test after two attempts. The one and only time she ever got drunk was at the celebration party the neighbors gave her the following weekend. It was as though there was a collective, "Thank God, the driving lessons are over."

Mom and Gladys remained good friends until Gladys passed away in 1999 from Multiple Sclerosis. Mom visited her often through her last years bringing baked goods and helping Gladys as best she could, and as much as Gladys would allow.

Mom never touched a cigarette to her own lips denouncing Dad's smoking as a filthy habit. Yet, she held many a cigarette up to Gladys' lips when Gladys could no longer maneuver her fingers on her own. These two women were always there to support one another.

Mom continually asked whoever would listen in any given situation, "Am I going to be okay?" It bothered the hell out of all of us. However, when I was that young, being able to help my Mom feel better was one of the first thrills of my life. It was gratifying to hear her say, "Oh, Debbie, thank you. I don't know what I'd do without you!" In that moment, she needed me.

{ ✹ }

CHAPTER TWO

When the Doctor Called

MEMORIES PLAYED OUT IN MY MIND AS I DROVE THROUGH THE ROLLING hills of Pennsylvania to see my parents the summer of 2012. They were in their late 70's and lived in a senior high rise in Clifton Park, New York. On that warm day in early July, those memories mixed with what I was imagining would lie ahead as Mom was struggling with the end stages of Congestive Heart Failure.

DRIVING HAS ALWAYS AFFORDED ME THE CHANCE FOR CREATIVE thinking. I thought about how being "nice" wasn't something that came naturally to Mom, especially when we were all young. No filters, no subtleties, what was in her head came out of her mouth. As I got older, it became apparent that I bothered the hell out of her. I was a very anxious, needy little girl, and I cried often. I can tell by looking at some of the photos of me that I was uncomfortable, afraid and sad. I got used to Mom being harsh with all of us, although I continued to yearn for a loving mother. She tried to enjoy motherhood but when I was six, she had twin girls; fifteen months later, she had Dave; and seven years later, Dina. The mother I knew for those first six years was long gone.

By the time I was eight, most things I did bothered both my parents. With three babies in 15 months, stress mounted every day, and Mom and Dad fought bitterly. They didn't need another person to care for, just someone to help out. Most things I did were a target for nasty, frustrated comments. If I continued to be silent and help them, I would be okay.

Throughout the years, I hoped I would do something or at least enough of everything to get a nod of approval. Dad was quicker to acknowledge an accomplishment than Mom. When I was able to get all the kids ready for church so we could be a half hour early for services or if I got all the kids' hair washed in the kitchen sink before their bedtime, he thanked me.

When I was in elementary school, Dad had high hopes for academic excellence for me. That didn't happen. Mediocre was the best I could do after 4th grade. I was a good reader in first and second grade, but when math was introduced, things changed and it all got harder for me. When dinner was over, and the table was cleared, Dad attempted to help me with multiplication. He gritted his teeth before he even sat down and I often started crying before we began the homework. This would frustrate and exhaust him and I felt like a failure. Not a good combination. Supposedly, Mom was excellent in math and would yell from the sofa in the other room, "I don't understand why you aren't good at math. I am." My anxieties were getting worse as a result of the stress of conditions at home.

> *Attention Deficit Disorder is a disorder where the children may be predominantly inattentive and, as a result, have great difficulty getting or staying focused on a task or activity. Little is taken into consideration when that diagnosis is given as to what is actually happening in the home that might be swirling around in that little kid's head at school. It's all about anxiety, all of it.*

With the level of stress felt by both of my parents, it is surprising they remained together and made it through. Now, looking back, I realize neither of them had anywhere else to go, or anyone who would take them in and they both knew it. Mom probably couldn't help but ridicule me every chance she got. Someone had to be on the receiving end of the hell she was living. She was fine with one child, but with four, she was nowhere near being okay, and we all knew it.

By the time Mom was in her late 70s, she had burned bridges with family, friends, and even strangers she and Dad met while walking the Rotterdam Park Mall. She could not have cared less. Dad became her constant and only companion through their later years. They seemed to have adjusted fairly well to his retirement in the early 90s, and neither could imagine life without the other.

The first time Mom was nice to me over the phone, I burst into tears. She said something along the lines of being proud of me. I was so shocked, I cried. About three years before she passed away, she started saying things I had yearned to hear for all fifty years of my life. Now, I couldn't handle it. I cried every time we spoke. I believed, like Julia Roberts' character said in the movie, *Pretty Woman,* "The bad things are easier to believe."

I called Dina almost wailing on the phone, "Mom's being nice to me!!!" Dina, 14 years younger than me, really didn't care. Dina lived up there near my parents. Maybe she was numb to it, because she and her husband, Adam, had rushed to our parent's aid many times during their later years. "It's the lower levels of oxygen in her blood. She's getting sicker," Dina said.

Oh my God!!! That was it! Had we known that lack of oxygen in Mom's blood was the answer to curbing her sharp, nasty, often obnoxious tongue, we could've rigged something up years ago!

As a direct result of lack of oxygen in Mom's blood stream, she and I began a journey back to how we had been with each other in the very beginning. She clearly knew who I was, and who we all were, but the disconnect gradually became more profound. As she was dying, this wasn't the woman to whom I had grown accustomed. She was more like a distant relative who had come to visit us and be nice.

With the onset of her symptoms, the early stages brought a myriad of doctor's appointments. Dad drove Mom to these in an attempt to find the source of her strange behavior. Their visits to several specialists proved unsuccessful. Dad told us and anyone else who would listen that there was nothing wrong with Mom. He spouted out that all these doctors only wanted their money. Mom was fine. The heart specialist who treated both my parents in their later years, as well as Mom's kidney specialist, were both excellent physicians. They came to understand that our parents were unwilling participants in any information that dared to invade their shared denial.

Dad kept the truth from us for a very long time. Only when Mom and Dad's general physician in Delanson, Dr. Burton, was able to get a "next of kin" phone number from Mom did any of us truly find out what was happening to her.

Every time any of the doctors asked for information, Dad filled out the papers. He sat in on every examination and refused to allow anyone to know what was going on. He was the only "next of kin" as far as he was concerned. He had to have control of this world of denial they were in, and Mom became increasingly passive allowing him to take over completely. That was the biggest red flag of all. She was no longer fighting back.

During an office visit, Dr. Burton asked Dad to leave the room to find a particular nurse Mom liked. It was only then that Dr. Burton convinced Mom to give her a "next of kin" phone number. Mom gave her mine.

Dr. Burton called me, surprising me, somewhat later in the evening. She introduced herself and said she wanted to go over Mom's case. I had nothing to go on, as far as the odd behaviors Mom was having, as Dad denied that anything was wrong. All five of us children thought Mom only had some mild form of dementia. Dr. Burton began to fill me in on the saga of dealing with my parents. She shared with me that she had called Dad earlier that evening to remind him to bring Mom's medicines for their appointment the next day. There was one question she asked at the beginning of our conversation that was the real shocker, "Does your father drink?" I told her that we had all joked about not calling them after a certain time at night because he sounded odd and wouldn't remember the conversation the following day.

"Your father and I had a conversation about your mother's medication, and he was slurring his words," Dr. Burton said. "He sounds very inebriated and I fear for your mother's safety if he is the one in charge."

She told me there were several times she had called them after office hours. Often, he sounded as though he had been drinking. Ethically, she had to find someone to bring into the situation since Dad was the one dispensing the medications.

The truth about Mom's health, Dr. Burton stated to me, was that she had been diagnosed with Congestive Heart Failure the year before. Dad, in an effort to protect Mom, had kept all this information from her, refusing to tell a soul.

Denise and Diana, my twin sisters, and Dina, along with their husbands, were diligently checking in on our parents throughout this time. Although, none of them lived close to Delanson, they took turns cleaning, cooking, and taking care of whatever rescue was required so Mom and Dad could remain living in the family home. Dad never hesitated to cry out for help to family or neighbors as he always expected to be rescued, no matter the inconvenience to others, which infuriated me.

The historic flood in 2010 that devastated areas of the Schoharie Valley was dangerously close to where Dina lived. Warnings were for people in her area to remain home, as the roads were dangerous. One of the main bridges had broken apart and washed down the Erie Canal in Rotterdam Junction. Some people had already drowned in low-lying areas near them.

As water was rising all around, Dad had called Dina, asking her to drive out to help him with his sump pump in the basement. He had flooding. Dina had called the twins to ask them what she should do. Everyone had forbidden her to drive out there, but she and her husband drove out anyway. Dad's flooding was minimal. They got the sump pump working again and drove back to their house, barely making it home.

Armed with the truth about Mom's health, I called each of my sisters and my brother, Dave, in California. Things were far worse with Mom than we had known. We began making decisions for Mom and Dad as they continued living in their version of reality. They resisted many of our suggestions, mainly our idea they should move to something smaller and easier to keep clean. Denise and Diana, who each had to drive over an hour to get to Delanson, did the things Mom and Dad would accept such as cleaning and shopping. Mom had lost interest in those things long ago. Blatantly, my parents refused to participate in what might lay ahead for them. Denial, blaming, secrecy; this was addiction at its finest.

CHAPTER THREE

The Beginnings of Wanderlust

Psychologist Eric Erikson, in his theory of human growth and development, stated there are eight profound stages we go through physically and emotionally from birth until our deaths. The first and most important, Trust vs. Mistrust, is central to our emotional well-being. There is conflict to be resolved within the first days of an infant's life. Until about 18 months, the infant searches faces and the environment to decide whether he can trust what he has been born into or not. "Am I going to be okay?" is answered by how the infants' needs are met, physically and — equally or more importantly — emotionally. Is there a connection between the infant and mother or a bond making the belonging between the two irreversible? If this first level involves an inconsistent or negligent connection from caregivers, emotional stability is fractured within a time of extremely vulnerable development. The reality of emotional struggles in infancy, that, in turn, later present themselves as anxiety, are "born" in this initial stage of seeking safety.

I HAVE A FEELING THAT LAUNCHING OFF INTO THIS FIRST LEVEL OF trust vs. mistrust didn't go so well for me. I believed I was going to be okay only if I was at the farm with Grandma Cecelia nearby. When I was born my parents lived with my grandparents, as did Dad's other two brothers. They all shared one bathroom. The farm was not big, and the bathroom was in my grandparent's bedroom, which they relinquished to my parents before I was born.

I heard rumors that once I came along, Mom had a strict code she abided by that no one was to go in and pick me up no matter how hard or long I cried. That was possibly some Dr. Spock thing. Grandma begged Mom to let her go in and sooth me, but she always said, "No." Apparently, Mom had an argument with one of my uncles and the next day we were out of there. She found a small second floor flat to rent in the village of Delanson, around the corner from where she grew up.

Mom, Dad and I lived in this tiny, dark, second floor flat in a dilapidated, old home behind the post office, in an alleyway called Elm Street. My crib barely fit into the smallest room, which was across from the main door into the apartment. That door opened onto a small landing and down a set of dark, steep stairs leading to the main floor where the landlords lived.

Our new landlords were Mr. and Mrs. Netherways, which I could only pronounce as "Otherways." I began my attempts to escape our apartment by climbing out of the crib, crawling, sometimes falling, down the dark, steep stairs to the Netherway's apartment door. "Otherways, Otherways, let me in!" I cried. I banged on their door until someone came to help me. I was trying to find my way back to my grandmother, where I knew emotionally, even at that very early, intensely vulnerable age, that I was going to be okay if I was with her.

Mom would joke about finding I had climbed out of my crib and ended up downstairs at the landlord's apartment door. She got several phone calls from Mrs. Netherways wanting to know if she knew where I was. "Yes, of course, I do," Mom would state with confidence. "She's in her crib taking a nap." I began my wanderlust of seeking out others at that old apartment. Mrs. Netherways informed Mom that I had been outside her door banging and shouting, "Mrs. Otherways, Mrs. Otherways, let me in! " Mom laughed as Mrs. Netherways explained I was now sitting naked on her dining room table. Mom loved telling tales of my leaving the apartment without her even knowing and, sometimes, with nothing on but a diaper.

One of the neighbors on the street of that old apartment called telling Mom he just happened to look out his window and saw me toddling down Post Office Hill. I have an idea where I was headed, but that is another story for a different book. How could she not hear me opening the door and heading out of the apartment? Years later, when I asked her about that, Mom said in an irritated voice, "Oh, I knew the one time you had gotten out because I heard you falling down the stairs." I could imagine Mom being totally annoyed to have her nap interrupted and being bothered that she had to go downstairs to bring me back. What I find amazing is how dedicated I must have been to escaping. I had to navigate those steep stairs down and out of the house, then continue down a long set of outside cement stairs to the alley road called Elm Street. I was born with a wanderlust that, even now, continues to inspire me to have a suitcase packed in case there is somewhere to go.

When I wasn't trying to escape, I often sat in my high chair making friends with the little girl on the package of Sunbeam Bread. She was blonde and pretty and always there. She and I were in a world of our own most of the day. I had a connection with or a type of attachment to inanimate objects which lessened my anxiety because I created my world around them. As I got older, I desired desperately to be out in the world doing my own thing. But, as an 18-month old, it required an ability to retreat into a world much more loving and safe. Was I going to be okay? Yes, little Sunbeam girl was there with me.

Since our bathroom was a converted closet with only a sink and toilet, Mom and I occasionally journeyed downstairs to use the Netherway's bathtub. I have fleeting memories of laughing with Mom in their tub. Now, it seems strange to imagine that she and I were regular visitors to the Netherways' bathtub, but Mom must have set something up so we could make our way into their lives as well. Mom loved being with older people. Most of the friends she and I visited were older couples who thought Mom was special, and I was adorable.

For my first six wonderful years, Mom and I had each other mostly to ourselves. I loved her with all my heart and, aside from my occasional escape from my crib, we spent every day, all day, together. At that time, as far as I knew, everything was going to be okay. Dad was an occasional visitor to our intimate reverie. He was six feet tall, very muscular and looked intimidating next to Mom's 4'11", 105-pound frame. His cold, blue eyes could glare right through me especially when he was thunderously and unpredictably impatient and intolerant. Fueled by non-filter Camel cigarettes, black coffee, and whiskey, he would blow up in anger when anyone had a look he didn't like. When I chanced to meet relatives later in my life, at reunions or weddings, they told me that Mom and Dad fought bitterly ever since they first met in the seventh grade. They said Mom had her eyes set on him from the very beginning and when she told Dad she liked him, he punched her. They didn't actually start dating until sometime in their junior year when they were both 16 years old.

Neither of my parents was passive. Both were aggressive. One aunt told me that when Mom and Dad first got married, they lived in a tiny apartment in the small town of Esperance. She and her husband, Uncle Floyd, lived on the same street. When walking down to my parent's apartment to visit, she could hear them screaming at each other from down the block. She would turn around and go home. This is the relationship into which I was born on June 6, 1957.

> *No one can predict how the event of a birth will change everything. So, how does one cope with insurmountable, overwhelming, unpleasant emotions? We do what we have seen our parents or caretakers do to cope.*

When I was grown and had children of my own, Mom told me that Dad had never wanted children. He wanted all of her attention for himself. However, Mom's sisters-in-law were having babies and she wanted one of her own.

I remember many kindnesses from both of my parents in those early years. Yet, there was always the underlying current of anger and resentment from both of them toward whomever was the target of hate on a particular day. Mostly, it was to one another. So, I became accustomed to feelings of chronic fear and panic. Eventually, anxiety was as familiar as the air around me. My parents acted like two small children fighting in a sandbox, "I'm more important!" "No, I am!" Within this world where I grew up, most days were tumultuous but some days were less frightening and I could relax and enjoy myself.

In most of my early photos I see a great deal of discomfort and fear in those sad brown eyes of mine. If Mom and Dad weren't spewing words of cruelty and hate to one another, they took on a poor, unknowing soul to judge, chastise and tear apart. The people they chose to rip apart, sometimes on a daily basis, were my beloved relatives whom I adored and with whom I felt the safest. There was only one person they left above their wrath, Grandma Cecelia Neadle.

CHAPTER FOUR

The Neadle Farm

CECELIA GRIESSMER NEADLE, MY FATHER'S MOTHER, WAS A "SAINT" as was stated by all who knew her. Her adult children, their spouses, and friends alike saw her inner strength, courage, and devotion to God and family. She and Grandpa Fabian Neadle lived on "The Farm" on Route 30 in Esperance, where they had moved as a family in 1948. Initially, they had lived in a small house renovated from a garage in Rotterdam, New York. Dad often said his father wanted to live on a farm so badly that he had a cow in the backyard behind the garage. On Floral Avenue, in Rotterdam, Grandma Cecelia's seven other brothers and sisters lived with their families. By the time they moved to the farm in 1948, Grandma Cecelia and Grandpa Fabian had five children, the youngest not quite two years old.

My guess is that Grandpa Fabian, who was not such a social guy, wanted to live out in the middle of nowhere, away from all the relatives. He and Grandma Cecelia found a farm that was 30 miles away from Rotterdam. She didn't want to move so far from her sisters and brothers who lived close to one another. With them, she could find love and support, which she desperately needed. According to Uncle Leon, Dad's youngest brother, and a beloved soul to me, they had moved from the comforts of the city to a place with an outhouse and no running water. It was a brutal existence. Grandpa Fabian's need to be on a farm, isolated away from people, created a life for his family, which, as Uncle Leon, described, was constant work. Grandma Cecelia got up at four each morning, chopped wood for the old iron stove and primed the manual pump at the sink which brought water from the outside well into the house. Then, she called upstairs to the four boys to get up and out to the barn. They had not been trained for this lifestyle. We never heard much at all about Grandpa Fabian's daily participation in all of this.

Grandma Cecelia was born on February 24, 1908, to Anthony and Francis Greissmer. Her father was a brutal German man who demanded that no one eat a meal until he had finished his and left the table. Her mother, Francis, was a warm, loving, sweet woman who suffered greatly at the hands of her husband. She raised her children as best she could.

In my teen years, Aunt Noreen, my father's sister, shared with me that Grandma Cecelia made sure the farm was always a warm and comforting place for her family to visit. I certainly felt that way. There were always aromas from the kitchen where we often found soup simmering on the stove. Even now, the smell of onions and celery cooking in butter instantly brings me back to that kitchen. I loved standing on a stool next to Grandma as she stirred the pot.

Grandpa Fabian Neadle was born April 4, 1903, to Arnold and Sophie Neadle in Ogdensburg, New York. There is family lore that Grandpa Fabian was traumatized at the age of 21 when his mother passed away, and his father remarried. The Neadle family originated in Montreal but when Grandpa Fabian's father and uncles had a bitter dispute, his father, Arnold, and his brother immigrated to Ogdensburg, very close to the Canadian border. Once in the United States, they changed their last name from La Boussiere, a beautiful French name meaning compass needle, to Needle. Then, they had a falling out, and Arnold changed the spelling from Needle to Neadle and remained estranged from all of his family.

Grandpa Fabian was odd. As beloved as Grandma was to me, Grandpa was scary. He rarely smiled. Looking today at photos of him, he usually had a blank stare or an angry look. When he and Grandma married, he was not everyone's favorite. Interestingly enough, that is how Grandma and Grandpa felt about Dad marrying Mom. Tales I heard of Grandpa Fabian were about the arguments he had with people. It seemed he was unable to get along with anyone, lost all his jobs and was very anti-social. In today's world, we might look at that as Aspergers, Autism, or Addiction. His most defining characteristics were being extremely defensive and paranoid, thinking that people were always talking about him.

Mom said one day Grandma Cecelia took all of her daughters-in-law and daughter, Noreen, to the barn and told them not to let her sons bully them into having sex like Grandpa Fabian did her. Even when they had company, Grandpa would take Grandma aside asking for sex. If she said no, Grandpa would storm out of the house and not return until the company had gone. It was difficult for Grandma to deal with him and his constant need for attention.

CHAPTER FIVE

The Lost Neadle

I WAS TOLD THAT OF ALL THE SIBLINGS, DAD IS MOST LIKE HIS FATHER. His brothers, Bernie, Ronnie, and Leon, appear less violent and his sister, Noreen, was the one who kept the family together in the years ahead. Everyone loved to go to Grandma Cecelia's. My cousins and I played there together most weekends when we were young and it all seemed wonderful. I remain close to my cousins today. Although we mostly live in different parts of the country, we remain in contact and faithful to our memories of Grandma Cecelia and our early times together.

Dad was employed in the Union of Steel Workers, which laid him off from November until May each year. Like his father, he tended to be unable to get along with people. Dad was one of only a few men willing to get into the massive cranes, called "cherry pickers," which were out on the barges on the Erie Canal. He maneuvered the crane to set massive steel beams on the locks that needed repair. He really enjoyed what he did, yet his undoing was that he didn't like being told what to do. He took things personally that were said to him and often reacted negatively to his supervisors.

He was always tight-lipped about his childhood, only saying that when he was a kid his father always thought people were talking about him. Grandpa Fabian would beat Dad and his brothers when they were laughing at the dinner table or in the living room, believing they were making fun of him. Dad told us about the time he asked his mom for socks for Christmas and how bad he felt when she started crying because there was no money for any presents that year. Those were the Depression years and they were barely able to feed themselves and the animals on the farm.

On Saturday, November 4, 1950, Dad, who was 16 years old, and his older brother, Ron, began a morning of hunting in the Adirondacks. They hiked the Northville/Placid trail near Benson, New York and planned, if they got separated, to meet at the beginning of the trail at 12 noon. It was a chilly November morning, and Dad had brought only a light jacket and didn't bother to bring matches or a compass as it was going to be a short hunt in an area they knew well. Dad saw a buck not too far ahead, just off the hiking trail, and he tracked it for a few hours. Finally, after losing sight of the deer, he decided to return to the trail

Fog had settled in and without a compass, Dad became disoriented and had no idea which way to go. It was beginning to get late and was long past the time he was supposed to meet Ron. Dad shot a few rounds into the air with his rifle to alert Ron as to where he was. The weather, which was calm that morning, had turned to bitter cold rain forcing Dad to find a spot under a couple of trees to sit out the rain. When no one showed up as a result of his gunshots, he became fearful, realizing he was lost.

Dad began to cry hysterically, unable to calm down. What if no one came to find him? He would be all alone in the woods that night. On edge and filled with terror, he heard a voice deep down inside. It sounded as if it was his father's voice, and he knew he had to straighten up and pull himself together if he was going to survive. He got up, and walked in the pouring rain in the direction he had previously chosen.

Later, he realized he had taken a wrong turn by going left instead of right. If he hadn't done that, he would have been out of the woods in 2-1/2 miles. Instead, he walked in the wrong direction for several hours and ultimately, found a dry place on the forest floor where he slept.

The next morning, Dad walked along the same trail drinking water from a stream that ran alongside the trail. Sunday turned into Monday with no sights or sounds of another person coming to his aid. The weather continued to rain…drizzles turned into torrential downpours. Dad kept walking the trail, knowing it would eventually end up somewhere. Later in the afternoon of his third day in the woods, Dad came upon a lean-to called Mud Pond. In the Adirondacks, the forest rangers maintain lean-tos along hiking trails for shelter.

Dad found a box of Spaulding's donuts wrapped in a bag and hanging on a cable, to protect it from wildlife. He was overjoyed and relieved to find food, matches to start a fire, a camp coffee pot, and coffee grounds. He later said that the coffee tasted like ice cream to him, grounds and all. There was fresh straw laid on the floor of the lean-to and he was able to really rest for the first time since his journey began.

Hundreds of men from surrounding areas in the Adirondacks and communities near where Dad lived came out in droves to search for the "lost Neadle youth," as he was called in every newspaper in that part of New York. Dad's parents and siblings went up to Avery's, a lodge which is nearby the beginning of the North/Placid trail. This lodge was where search parties gathered, rested, and had food. Dad's parents anxiously waited there, never leaving until he was found.

Along with a helicopter that General Electric provided, there were five single-engine planes used in the search each day. Men held hands in rows of 25 to 50, covering as much ground as they could. By day four, all hopes were lost that they would find Dad alive. His brother was beside himself with guilt that he was unable to find Dad. School was canceled in many districts so that students and teachers could aid with the search.

Tuesday, Dad began his fourth day of walking the trail alone. He felt great. Along with the donuts and coffee in the lean-to, Dad had found potatoes and clean socks. That night, he came upon his second lean-to called Canary Ponds, where he stayed until morning. Again, he found food and clean socks. Having gathered strength from two good night's rest, Dad set out on Wednesday, his fifth day lost, to continue walking with the hope of rescue.

Sometime around 11 a.m., Dad saw two men coming towards him on the trail. They came up and asked him if he had seen anyone in the woods as they were looking for a lost kid named Richard Neadle. "I'm Richard Neadle," he said.

Within 30 minutes, they had fed him his favorite sandwich of baked beans and ketchup, walked out of the woods, and got into their 1946 Ford Coupe to start the journey back to the lodge. Those two men were Bruce Bush and Ted Farnsworth. Dad remembered them for the rest of his life. He said the scariest thing about the whole experience was the wild ride those guys gave him to Avery's Lodge. Everyone who was waiting could see Dad was not only alive, but quite well.

When the news of Dad's being found alive and well reached Delanson, fire whistles blew and church bells rang. Villages and towns like Esperance, Duanesburg and even Arietta, New York, the area where Dad finally walked out of the forest, had fire hall dances and gave gratitude.

The following spring, the Duanesburg Central High School yearbook featured a poem about Dad:

THE LOST NEADLE

You've heard of the needle the haystack concealed
From every searching eye,
But do you know of the one the mountains hid?
If not, to tell you, I'll try.

The woods near Canada Lake was the place
One Saturday morn, the time,

The "Neadle", you've guessed, was in search of deer
Though cold and damp was the clime.

The deer eluded this hunter
And so did the trail he sought.
Time passed when he was supposed to return
But no glimpse of him was caught.

So men from miles around set out
To tramp through mountain and bog
To seek some trail that would lead them to
The hunter lost in the fog.

His teachers and schoolmates, determined to help
Laid books and work aside.
The school was closed, forgotten now
'Til they, their hands had tried.

Saturday, Sunday, Monday, and Tuesday
Such hunting men never had done
On foot, by plane, by ladders in caves
Each day ending as it had begun.

No track, no clue, no trace was found
And still the search was waged
While coffee and food the women prepared
So hunger would be assuaged.

And then the joyful news was brought
The sirens blew the call,
"Dickie is found, the search is o'er
Return now, one and all.

And people at home by their radios
Heard with joy the tidings,
"Found at last alive and well
Safe from the mountains' hidings."

> So, instead of the haystack of old renown
> That hid the needle from view,
> T'was the Adirondack Mountains this time
> To our 'Neadle's' trail held the clue.
>
> As far as we know, no one ever has found
> That elusive needle in the hay,
> But everyone knows the "Neadle" in the mountains
> Was found one Gladsome day.

This event solidified for Mom her need to have Dad in her life. She felt if she had him, she wouldn't ever be alone again. Each day while he had been missing, she had felt abandoned. From that time forward, Mom did whatever she needed to do to keep Dad close to her.

When Dad was in his 80s, and his memory began to fail him, he was unable to remember much of what happened on the same day. Yet, if he was asked about this episode of his life, all names, dates, and facts were as clear in his mind as the days of the adventure. In fact, he would point out that this adventure was the reason he never went anywhere from that time forward without his waterproof matches.

CHAPTER SIX

Where Abandonment Came From

DRIVING ALONG THE LONG LONELY STRETCH OF HIGHWAY FROM ERIE to Buffalo in that summer of 2012, I thought about how my relationship with Mom had changed and shifted so much throughout the years. It was unimaginable that we would not have her with us. There is no way to prepare for what lay ahead especially knowing Mom might have more anxiety and panic than ever. I didn't know what had happened that made Dina say I should come, but it couldn't be good.

Whenever I asked Mom if I was going to be okay, she would frown and say either "Oh, yes" or more often, "How am I supposed to know?" Neither was particularly soothing, leaving a permanent flow of uncertainty.

The survival tactic I used while growing up in the smaller version of World War II that was recreated in my house on a nightly basis was to go to my room and lose myself completely in a book, or a television show. Sometimes, I would re-enact a movie I had just seen. I struggle to this day to stay in reality and not become, in some part, a character I have just read about or taken from a show. This escape was my first form of coping with years of horrific insults from Dad to Mom, "You dirty guinea. Italian low life bitch." And, in response, Mom would have a constant flow of "You Nazi bastard. You would kill us all if you could!" Through the years, we children were the dining room table audience to this. There were times when it seemed Dad could do that very thing – kill us all. In fact, in photos of my father as a little tyke in the mid to later 1940s, he had a similar look to that of Hitler youth.

I garnered an intense interest in the Holocaust in my teen years, reading anything I could get my hands on about the survival of the persecuted during the war. It was as though these were primer books on how to continue living. My parents were horrifying and dangerous emotionally to be around. Their arguments, which took place during my early youth right up to Mom's death, sent terror into my heart even with all my years of therapy. Having been alone with them for my first six years, I had witnessed their series of brutal verbal fights, and somehow felt responsible. I had been too young to understand that none of it was my fault. The most upsetting part of growing up in this type of environment was that I loved them both. I cried often and was ridiculed and shamed for it. They looked at me from their violent rages and bellowed, "And, what the hell is wrong with you? What are you crying about?"

Mom loved to tell her story of being orphaned at the age of three, sent to live with her grandmother, then a series of foster homes until she was finally placed in a permanent home. I heard it often since I was the only one interested in listening. She would always add that she was "the little girl who no one wanted."

Actually, very little is known about Mom's parents, Gabriel and Josephine Mastroianni. My grandfather immigrated to the United States from Naples, Italy, sometime in 1930 to live with an uncle and find work. He processed through Ellis Island and then took the train up to Schenectady, New York, where General Electric was employing thousands of immigrants who were desperate for work.

In the late 20s and early 30s, there was a major influx of Italian, Polish and German immigrants who had just come off the boats. They were more than happy to take even the most degrading jobs.

Not long after he arrived, Gabriel met a girl named Josephine, who never learned how to read or write. It appeared she had undiagnosed intellectual disabilities and, supposedly, was married off as soon as possible when Gabriel was 32 and Josephine 16. Mom's oldest brother, Tom, was told they had to get married because Josephine was pregnant with him. My mother, Judith Marie, was born a year later in December of 1933. Within seven years, there were five little children with a husband who hardly worked and was as demanding as a dictator.

Grandma Josephine's father, Thomas Zullo, gave Grandpa Gabriel a gas station to run, but he was not interested in working or being told what to do. He went through a series of jobs, which led their growing family to move as many times as they had children.

At the age of three, my mom became sick with Rheumatic Fever. Grandma Josephine couldn't handle taking care of a sick child along with all the other babies in a one-bedroom apartment, so she took Mom away from her siblings and dropped her off at her mother's apartment like an unwanted bag of clothes. The oft-told story involved Mom and Grandma Josephine walking hand in hand down the sidewalk from their family apartment to Mom's grandmother's apartment. Once at Mary's apartment, Grandma Josephine let go of Mom's hand and left her there. The story goes that Mom didn't see her siblings or parents again for over two years.

> If accuracy is based on perception, as most researchers will tell you, a traumatic event may be remembered quite differently than what actually happened.

Uncle Tom challenged Mom's memory in later years when visiting our home in Delanson. When talking about what happened in their childhood, he insisted that she had not been "taken away." He said she went to stay with their grandmother only three blocks away and they visited each other often. Yet, she remembered it as though she had been a sickly, unwanted, three-year-old child.

General Electric was in its heyday at that time with all its soot and pollution spread throughout Schenectady. Grandma Mary used to walk Mom by the Mohawk River that ran through Schenectady because she believed the moist air by the river would help Mom breathe. For the year or so that Mom lived with her grandparents, life was stable and she became attached to Grandma Mary. By this time, the remainder of Mom's siblings, Gabriel, Margaret, and Marlene, were born.

Grandma Josephine was becoming overwhelmed with having to care for four children. The youngest, Marlene, was just six months when Grandma Josephine finally asked her mother if she could come home to live. She reported Grandpa Gabriel was beating her and even refused to let her listen to the radio. Mom had very few memories of her mother and didn't remember ever being held or loved. The one memory she had of her father was of him yanking the radio plug out of the wall socket and throwing the radio against a door, shattering it. Grandma Mary refused to allow Grandma Josephine to come back home because she believed a woman must remain with her husband and children.

There are variations on exactly what happened to push Grandma Josephine over the edge. Most likely, as is normally the case, it was a combination of a lot of things. Uncle Tom remembers his mother taking all four children to the police station, which was close to their apartment, to find safety from the abuse of her husband. They were allowed to stay for one night in a small room at the police barracks but were sent home the next morning. There was nowhere for Grandma Josephine to go for shelter forcing them all to return to Grandpa Gabriel.

Grandma Josephine had often babysat for a family who lived in the apartment above theirs and had become very close to them. She confided in them about the hell she was living. When the neighbors informed her they were moving to Harrisburg, Pennsylvania, they invited her to leave with them. In the middle of the night, Grandma Josephine slipped out of the apartment and ran away.

Grandpa Gabriel went into a tirade because his wife had left him and the children. He stormed down to Grandma Mary's home and took Mom away for he wanted nothing to do with Josephine's family. Grandpa Gabriel couldn't care for all those small children by himself in the tiny apartment, so within a few days, the Catholic Church found places for all of them in St. Coleman's Children's Home in Albany. There, Mom slept on a small cot with her sister, Maggie, who was a year younger, and Marlene, the youngest, was left crying in a crib somewhere in another room. This home was later investigated regarding the deaths of several children that occurred during the 1930s and 1940s.

Mom's sisters remained in St. Coleman's until they came of age, while the boys were sent to a private all boys prep school. Sadly, none of the children had the chance to be adopted into happy homes as Grandpa Gabriel refused to relinquish his rights as a father. So, the children remained wards of the Catholic Church.

St. Coleman's was unable to care for Mom as her Rheumatic Fever became worse due to the substandard living conditions of the orphanage. She was taken away from her siblings one last time and put into a series of foster homes. There were many families who tried to take care of Mom, but none lasted very long. This was when she developed the belief that she was "the little girl who no one wanted." Being so young when she experienced this trauma, she remained that emotionally frightened child for the rest of her life.

CHAPTER SEVEN

Surviving Aunt Rose

IN 1939, CATHOLIC CHARITIES PLACED AN ADVERTISEMENT IN THE Schenectady Gazette in hopes of finding a home for Mom. Anthony and Rose Casile of Delanson, originally from Stromboli, Italy, saw the advertisement and answered it. They decided to take in another foster child.

Rose Canastra Casile had come from Stromboli, along with her parents and all of her seven younger siblings, to a small town called Worcester, New York. Rose married Tony, and they bought a farmhouse in Delanson in the late 1920s so Tony could find employment working on the railroad.

A two-mile long road, once called Toad Hallow Road, now Highway 395, meandered through a valley between the major routes of 7 and 20. Delanson was once known as Toad Hallow and was renamed when the Delaware and Hudson Railroad built a main crossing station in the middle of this tiny hamlet. They took Del from Delaware, an from and, son from Hudson and there it was…Delanson. No more Toad Hallow.

Aunt Rose and Uncle Tony, as Mom was instructed to call them, moved into the old farmhouse on Wilson Street, a dead end off Post Office Hill in the village. When Rose and Tony first moved to the farm, their two-year-old daughter, Mary, got sick as a result of drafts from when they tore up part of the house to remodel. She developed pneumonia and later died. Guilt or anger over Mary's death played a role in how Aunt Rose harshly treated everyone, except her son, Anthony.

Stories of Aunt Rose's hatred-filled rants were legendary. She seemed to hate all girls equally but pampered Anthony. When there was not enough milk to go around for the foster kids, there was still some for Anthony. He stayed at his music teacher's house rarely coming home until after 8 p.m. throughout his childhood. Mrs. Van Schoick was his music teacher who was preparing him for classical training and, most likely, treated him less oppressively than his mother. He was out of the house and off to Julliard School of Music by the time Mom came to live there.

Mom was part of a small group of girls from Catholic Charities who lived at Aunt Rose's along with several of her actual nieces whose mothers had died. For a time, everyone lived upstairs, except for Rose, Tony, and Anthony, who had been struck with polio when he was very young. It was a working farm, with mostly goats and chickens and a huge garden that Uncle Tony and the foster kids tended. Mom often shared stories about how kind, meek and mild Uncle Tony was.

Aunt Rose was harsh and cruel… making sure each girl knew she was NOT her mother. There was a large photo of Mary, the daughter

Aunt Rose had lost, hanging over the sofa as a constant reminder to Aunt Rose that none of the little girls who lived there was Mary. When Mom arrived, Aunt Rose took particularly good care of her and made sure she got the rest she needed due to the rheumatic fever. Aunt Rose's harsh nature came out after the fever subsided.

Eventually, Aunt Rose became an advocate for all the girls, Philly, Connie, Mom and Margo. She insisted they do well in school so they could have all the advantages that children who came from families within the village and surrounding areas would have. Yet, Mom's stories of her childhood were peppered with recounts of some of the harsh, abusive verbal and physical treatment that Aunt Rose dished out. She also told funny stories of the escapades of Aunt Rose's sisters and their drunken father, who all lived upstairs together.

When Mom was nine, Aunt Rose hit her on the head with the heel of a shoe as she was going out a door. She left the house crying and went to the home of her best friend, Ellen Dutcher. They usually walked to and from school together and that day, Ellen made her come inside to get a towel for the blood and show her mother what had happened. Ellen's mother was going to call Catholic Charities to report Aunt Rose, but Mom begged her not to. She didn't want to move to another foster home and have to get to know another family. So, she remained at the Casile's and learned to deal with it. Mom described growing up at Aunt Rose's as harsh, but fun due to the huge family all living together under one roof. She said Aunt Rose got nicer as she got older.

Philomena (Philly) Casile was four years older than Mom and had been living with Aunt Rose since she was about four years old. Her mother had died leaving Philly and her brother with a father who could not care for them, so Aunt Rose took them in. Mom attached herself to Philly as she had never done with anyone else and remained very close to Philly the rest of her life. Philly's children became our "cousins" in years to come.

From the beginning of Mom's first true stable home, Philly guided her in everything. Mom often said that Philly thought she was a pest but allowed her to tag along when Philly did big girl things. Two other girls, Connie and Margo, who were somehow related to Rose, lived there as well.

Mom loved taking Uncle Tony's lunch pail to him at his watchtower at the train stop in the middle of the village. She got into big trouble one day when Uncle Tony sent word to Aunt Rose that he didn't get his lunch. Mom had been daydreaming, skipping off into her own fantasy world, which, by that time, had been richly created with places she dreamed of and filled with people who loved her, and had forgotten to take it to him. She got a "lickin" and remembered to give Uncle Tony his lunch bucket every time after that.

Mom remained at Aunt Rose's house until her wedding day, October 1, 1955. She was loyal and steadfast in her devotion to her surrogate mother, even when Aunt Rose was bedridden with stomach cancer and said horrible, mean things to her from her deathbed. It didn't matter to Mom. Rose had taken her in and kept her.

Aunt Rose was heavy set, mean and smelly. She yelled at me for sucking my thumb, which I did until I was five. Mom defended me - the only time I remember her doing that - and told Aunt Rose I would eventually stop… which I did, around the time of Mom's driving lessons.

CHAPTER EIGHT

In and Out of Church

OUR LIVES REVOLVED AROUND OUR LADY OF FATIMA CATHOLIC Church. Mom and I were part of the Lady's Altar Society, responsible for cleaning the church. Each Saturday, I watched Mom, and the other young women reverently take the altar cloths off, and take them to the priest's house next door to clean them as the Catholic Diocese dictated.

This took place before Vatican II. Mass was said in Latin with the priest facing the wall behind the altar where the massive crucifix hung. All of that scared me. I didn't understand any of it. What impacted me the most was the total transformation of Mom's anxious state to one of peace, calm and serenity when she was in church. She was safe there, wrapped in the arms of the Virgin Mary, her one connection to the maternal. She would smile and sing, and I would get as close to her as she would allow, taking in her temporary gentleness. The kneeling risers were slightly cushioned, which made it hard for me to stand on them. I would try to get my balance on the kneeler, teetering close to Mom while she prayed, but careful not to break her reverie into the other daydream world where she seemed to go. Prayer was very important. She and I would say prayers before I went to bed at night, kneeling by the bedside, listing the names of all the people we needed to pray for after reciting Our Father and the Hail Mary.

That list flows through my memory to this day. I folded my little hands and bowed my head saying along with Mom, "God bless Grandma and Grandpa, Rosie and Tony, Gampa Gabriel, Father Joe," and the list continued on. I still say it in my head, pronouncing the names in the exact same way I did when I was three.

Grampa Gabriel died the year my parents got engaged, 1953. He died right after the holidays, suffering a heart attack as he got off a bus in downtown Schenectady. To me, he was someone important to Mom because she had added him to the very first part of all those who needed my prayers each night.

Through the years, as my siblings and I grew up, married and moved away, Mom and Dad became disillusioned with the Catholic Church. They had some falling out, of course, with one of the old, alcoholic priests that the Archdiocese farmed out to the smaller, less important parishes in Schenectady County. They heard rumors that this priest was having an affair with the church secretary, and all of it was too much for them. She and Dad occasionally went to church with one of us when we were grown, but they had long since quit attending church on a regular basis where they lived. They remained hateful of all they had once loved and revered in those beloved times of my life so long ago.

Whenever I am in a church or a cathedral, I immediately think of my mother. Tears come to my eyes as I remember how it all meant so much to us back then. Holidays were full of all the rituals with meanings, incense, and holy water. Above my parents' bed, there was a crucifix that had a small wooden door that slid upwards to reveal a little bottle of holy water. Mom told me that in case anyone died at home, the priest would have easy access to what would be most important in those last moments of life.

There were a few women from Our Lady of Fatima in Delanson with whom Mom had a connection. They were mostly women older than she was; mother figures to be sure, but also women able to handle her neediness and her inability to give back.

One such woman was Veronica Dubner. Her son, Stephen J. Dubner, author of *Turbulent Souls*, writes fondly of how caring his mother was with women from our church. Veronica helped many of the women who needed care and guidance. Mom was a perfect example. While I was attending Duanesburg Central High School, Mom often met Veronica, either at church to pray or up at Veronica's house to talk. Mom rarely had people at our house; she wanted to be the guest in their homes. Veronica nurtured my mother through times of severe anxiety by listening to her for hours, gently reminding her that God had her in His care.

Stephen Dubner was a classmate of my twin sisters, Denise and Diana. When they were in their junior and senior years, Denise's boyfriend was Richard LaPoint. Stephen resented Richard because he was the star basketball player. Stephen's attributes as an accomplished writer were never recognized in our tiny high school. Creativity, such as writing, acting or singing, was not highly rated at DCS; sports were. Interesting how life changes after high school. Stephen J. Dubner is now the star...an amazing author, journalist and reporter for the *New York Times*.

CHAPTER NINE

Things We Never Talk About

WHEN I WAS WITH GRANDMA CECELIA, I WAS ALWAYS GOING TO BE okay. She loved all of her grandchildren, and my very young heart believed that of all the cousins, she loved me best. I didn't know until many years later, Grandma knew how harsh my father treated people and she feared for us children. His temper and self-centeredness were well-known throughout the family. His rage struck terror in our lives, but while Grandma Cecelia was alive, we were safe.

Once, when I was brushing Grandma Cecelia's hair using an old mangled brush with a broken handle, I heard Mom say, "Debbie, Stop! You're hurting Grandma." She was lying down on the left side of the old green sofa in Grandma's living room. Her voice was harsh. "Your Grandma doesn't want you doing that."

"Judy, she's fine," said Grandma, allowing me the opportunity to be with her. I liked that. I loved being this close to Grandma, leaning against her. She smelled of Ivory soap, and I yearned for human touch.

Grandma Cecelia passed away when I was eight years old. Right before she died, Dad took me to see her one last time at the Cobleskill

Hospital. In those days, little kids couldn't go inside the hospital, so Dad told me to stay in the car and wait for Grandma to wave out the window. The twins were about a year old and were in the back seat, belted into a box as a car seat Dad had rigged up. I stepped out of the car when I saw her lean out of the window, waving at me. I was crying and yelling "Hi Grandma!" Her head was wrapped in a handkerchief and her sweet face was smiling. That was the last time I saw her.

Life after she died, changed drastically. Grandpa Fabian died a year before Grandma Cecelia so there were no more family gatherings at the farm. Now, Uncle Ronnie lived there alone. He was struggling as he was used to having Grandma Cecelia do everything for him. We were all lost without her and even though our house was only three miles from the farm, Mom didn't go visit there again for more than two years.

Childhood Trauma Timeline states from birth through the ages of five or six, our worth and value are formed by what we see, what we hear and, most importantly, how we are treated. Some might think the very early years of a person's existence are meaningless, but it is quite the opposite. Any trauma experienced within this age range, especially three through six, will alter the course of how we deal with life and how we feel about ourselves. If a young child experiences a death of a relative or close friend within these ages, rarely do adults take enough time to talk with the child about what happened and where that person went.

Growing up in our house, there was no showing of emotion by kids other than being happy, and even then, we needed to keep it to a minimum. No mistakes, no questions, and no neediness were ever to be shown. If there were temper tantrums, they were performed by my parents, especially Dad. Although I loved this man and learned so much from his strength and sense of humor, I was struck by terror when he got angry. We all were, except for Mom. It was possible that I was not going to be okay at all when he exploded in fury, and it escalated into points where no one knew if something really bad might happen.

When I was eight years old, I was at my friend's house playing in the basement when I heard a loud banging at their front door. It was my father. I didn't realize what time it was. I was supposed to have gone home sooner. Knowing nothing about social appropriateness, Dad dragged me out of their house. Then he started hitting me and continued beating me in front of neighborhood kids and neighbors looking out of their windows. He continued hitting me all the way down the street until we got to our house, all because I was late for dinner. When Mom and Dad exploded at the same time, we kids were uncertain if we would make it out alive.

One Sunday sometime in the spring, we went to a picnic to honor Uncle Bernie and Aunt Marilyn. Dad's oldest brother and his current wife. Bernie's first marriage was to Kay, whom she met right after coming home from the service in Korea. They had two children, Anne and Arthur, but they divorced when Arthur was about two. He then married Marilyn with three daughters of her own. At their reception, all of the cousins lined up on a bench for a photo. Marilyn's two older daughters seemed to hate everything about this new family. Each of them stood at either end of this line of cousins, holding one of my newborn twin sisters for the photo and they looked less than thrilled. I heard that when Uncle Bernie and Aunt Marilyn got married, Uncle Bernie had to carry the oldest daughter, kicking and screaming, into his house. We were young and thought they were just more cousins who had come to play.

By the time of this picnic, Grandma Cecelia and Grandpa Fabian had passed away within a year of each other. My safety and sanctuary were gone. It seemed that all the uncles and aunts floundered a bit after both grandparents had died, and, most assuredly, those in conflict with one another became even more estranged.

Earlier on that Sunday morning, I could hear Mom yelling and banging cupboard doors signaling us it was time to get up and get ready for church. Something had set her off. In the late 1960s, Sundays had a certain feel to them. Everything was quite different back then. No one dared speak out against authority like politicians, priests, teachers, parents - in our house, at least. When things happened that were scary or threatening at home, no one spoke of it. No one dared say anything outside of our house about how frightening it could be at times. Sunday's Catholic mass was at 8 a.m. for which we were always a half hour early. After mass, we came home and got ready for dinner and the dreaded Sunday drive. On this particular day, we left for the church before 7:30 a.m. I could tell my parents had already been arguing for Mom was in a strange black mood that bothered me more than it did anyone else. Then, after church, there was a bake sale and Mom bought a pie for the picnic. Once we pulled into the garage, which had a side door up a few stairs up into the kitchen, Mom got out of the car and accidentally dropped the pie. It was small incidents like this that sometimes turned into a holy war. Today was that kind of day. I could feel the tremors of hate from my mom toward all of us. She didn't want to spend another weekend with any of her in-laws. I was ten, the twins and David were three and two at that time. My heart was racing, and my whole body tensed as she ran into the house yelling and screaming. "I can't stand this anymore!" She banged the door open yelling, "I hate you, I hate you all!" Dad ran after her swearing in anger, leaving us all alone in the garage still in the car. We all sat in the back seat, the little kids crying and looking at me for help.

We stayed in the car for a few moments until Dad came back to the kitchen door, eyes red and bloodshot, face blotched from shouting, motioning us to come into the house. I didn't want to. Once in the house, I herded the kids into my room while Mom and Dad yelled and cried until they wore each other out. When it was quiet, the twins and Dave left my room and went into their own rooms to play. The fights were normally about Dad's relatives or money. I didn't know what it was about that day, but I knew I didn't want to get back in that car with them to go anywhere.

A few hours later, we all piled back into the car, leaving for Uncle Bernie's which was a short drive down the back, beautiful winding roads from Delanson to Esperance. Things between Mom and Dad were still tense. I couldn't get the sense of dread to go away. Both seemed on the verge of fighting again even as we got to Uncle Bernie's and began to intermingle with everyone there. Luckily, I was able to run off and play with some cousins. Several hours later, I heard my father's voice calling for us to all get in the car. We were leaving. Dad had a drink in one hand and a cigarette in the other. He was visibly mad. He and Mom were bickering even in front of the relatives. They didn't seem to care if there was an audience. I was mortified to see them at each other like this and seeing how the aunts and uncles who were saying goodbye to us had a look of concern. I didn't want to get in the car. I begged Dad to let me stay with my cousins, asking if maybe I could go home with Aunt Noreen. I loved it at her house with my cousins, Cathy and Karen. I was safe there. He looked at me with his cold blue eyes, now bloodshot, tossed his drink out and ordered me into the backseat with the rest of the kids.

I dreaded getting in that car. I sensed there was something even more wrong than earlier in the day. Mom was in a mental state where she seemed totally disconnected from all of us. I looked around hastily and saw my cousin, Anne, who was a year older than me, standing next to me. I asked her if she'd like to come home with us, not letting on that things were deteriorating between my parents. I made it sound like it'd be fun. I asked Dad and he didn't seem to pay attention to me but made a slight nod "yes." I thought my parents might behave if someone else was in the car. They did not. Once in the car, Dad pulled out onto McGuire School Road heading for home. My mother started to rant about all the asshole relatives at the picnic, and Dad spat out swear words and hateful rants of his own.

As we drove away from Uncle Bernie's house, Dad started to speed down the winding country road. I became lightheaded, and my heart was pounding out of control. I could feel our lives were in danger. Anne sat on one side in the backseat. I sat on the other side with the small kids between us, as Dad escalated in anger pushing further down on the gas pedal. I could see from the back seat that the car was going faster and faster as the trees flew past the car windows. I smelled the stale stink of alcohol as Mom was hatefully pointing out to him that he was, in fact, just a drunk and she hated him. My panic kicked in completely as the trees we passed were now a blur. Dad seemed to not care if we died in this car. I had to do something. I had never before said anything to my father when I wanted him to stop yelling or hitting me, but now I needed to save our lives, hopefully. The kids were crying, and when I looked over at Anne, she was frozen stiff in fear. She also had the look of dread and doom. I stood up right behind my father and pleaded with him, "Daddy, please slow down." The speedometer was steadily going up as he drove faster and faster. He put his massive fist up to my face while keeping his eyes on the road and bellowed, "Sit down and shut up!" I sat back down in my seat. I knew the kids were petrified. They were crawling on top of me. He kept going even faster down the road. My mother never stopped picking on him. She never shut up. They were going to kill us, and there was nothing I could do.

There was a slight rise in the road where McGuire School Road met Route 20. Miraculously, Dad started to slow the car down as the stop sign was just ahead. I couldn't believe I might not die. As we began to slow down even further, my mother opened her car door and jumped out. My heart was racing, my throat dry. I felt like throwing up. I just knew Mom was dead, or possibly lying in pain under the wheels of the car she had just escaped, possibly to save her life.

Dad screeched the car to a halt. He jumped out, and I watched as he picked Mom up off the ground and carried her to the farmhouse right near where we stopped. There was total silence in the car. Dad had left us in the car in the middle of the road.

We sat in the car for what seemed like a very long time. All of us looking at each other without making a sound, wondering what was going to happen now. I wouldn't look at Anne. I knew she was probably mad at me for asking her to come. From the horror we had just endured, I was sure something bad had happened to my mother. I saw Dad come out of the front door of the farmhouse carrying Mom back to the car. He opened the passenger side door and gently placed Mom in the car. It seemed odd. I had never before seen him so tender and caring toward her.

"Is she dead?" I asked. Dad looked up at me with the strangest expression as if he just then remembered that we were all left in the car. He said, "No." And, that was it. He drove home slowly and carefully.

Mom looked as though she was sleeping. There were no scrapes. There was no blood. She was just sitting there in the passenger seat with her head slumped to the left side. Dad said she wasn't dead so I figured she had fainted and was still out or possibly, being a bit of an actress herself, she was faking it!

When we were all safely home and in the house, I went to my room. I still couldn't believe I was alive. I felt as though I was being set free from them holding us hostage to their insanity.

Later, I ventured out to the living room where I saw my mother lying on her right side on the left corner of that sofa. She was reaching out her hand to Anne to hold as she said, "Isn't he a bastard?" It was a scene straight out of a bad B movie. Mom was the heroine who had survived the trauma. It struck me cold.

Anne stayed with Mom, continuing to hold her hand, as the three little kids huddled around Mom, quietly watching. Dad had gone to their bedroom. Never once did either of my parents ask if we were okay. Never. They showed no concern that we all had gone through one of the scariest rides of our lives. What I realized as I went back to my bedroom, was that I was alone in all of this. My siblings were mine to care for, especially emotionally.

From that day forward, I knew what I had to do. I set my jaw, clenched my teeth and held on. Clearly, neither parent knew how to be interested in our wellbeing. If children are to survive and thrive, they have to be considered. We were not. I knew my answer to being okay would be "NO" while I was living in their house. A kind of self-preservation grew within me as feelings of being overwhelmed, unsupported, and then abandoned, cycled through most days. Incidents like that car ride sent me into helplessness which seemed to me to be severe mental illness. There wasn't ever an apology for their actions and no accountability for the feelings of anyone around them. I tried not to show any signs of being jittery or anxious.

> It is no wonder that alcohol, drugs, eating, not eating, spending, sexing and gambling are the go-to stress releasers and coping mechanisms of our society. If we aren't having open, honest conversations with our children about what they see, hear, and how they are being treated, this will only intensify. The extreme of the early childhood trama is in direct correlation with the diagnosis. Any fact or evidence-based case study on these topics of mental illness, addiction, and grief, when delved into further, point to something happening that was so profoundly traumatizing for that family that it became the elephant in the room. When this happens, behaviors and beliefs can be passed down through generations. So, with the culmination of secrecy and time, there is no knowledge of where they came from or why.

Often, I heard Mom talk in a ridiculing, shameful way about people she knew who suffered nervous or mental breakdowns. It was a clear message to me that however I felt inside, no matter what, I had better keep it together. To appear "emotionally unbalanced" was something my parents watched for because for them mental illness was a horribly shameful thing. More and more, I felt as though I was walking on a tightrope ready to fall into the abyss of insanity at any moment.

After that car ride, I became overwhelmed with panic when it came time for the Sunday drive. From the time I was ten years old until about 15, when I was finally allowed to stay home, I had a chronic dread of Sundays. There was no saying "No" to either of them. The late 1960s was a time in the world when young people were beginning to speak out and protest, but not in my house. Not ever. So, how would I know to stand up for myself or that something was unacceptable if everything I saw and heard had to be accepted? Would I ever know the feeling of being loved and safe again as I had felt at the farm with Grandma? Would I ever be someone's favorite again?

I have emotionally revisited this trauma scene throughout my life. I wouldn't have the clear scene come to mind except the many panic attacks endured throughout my life were triggered by some form of speeding either in a car, on a boat, or a subway. Feelings of panic I've had in certain situations have brought the same physical feelings and emotions as I had that day. It took years of talking through my anxieties in therapy to realize this trauma scene really happened. It was never talked about again in our house...ever! As the years passed, I began to think it had been a dream. It wasn't. Years later, at a family reunion, I asked my cousin, Anne, if that car ride was something she remembered. She recalled, in horror, how she remembered the incident, as well. My emotions from this trauma had pushed the incident down, and it needed to be brought to the surface with a trusted therapist and finally healed.

CHAPTER TEN

Frightened and Barely Holding On

AFTER THAT DAY, MY DISILLUSIONMENT OF AND HATRED FOR MY mother took hold. It was as though someone had severed whatever cord connected me to her. It was apparent that Mom couldn't stand me either. Many of her hateful rants ring in my head still. I was a "no good God damn bitch." I would "end up pregnant by 16." End up "a nothing." Mom made these statements over and over again as I got older. My throat would close, and I felt the detachment, the doors closing inside me to the point of not knowing how to be with anyone else without attaching to them in a detached manner. The transition from those early years of being her everything to being despised by her took a toll that I struggle with still. No amount of therapy can erase those words of hate she rained down on me …more than anyone else. I can see now it was how she was raised and how Aunt Rose had treated her. I vowed never to say anything to my kids like what was said to me.

> The debate over whether addiction is caused by nature or nurture is ongoing. Some of us have a genetic predisposition to both mental illness and addiction, and research and statistics researchers still think it's about 50/50. Genetics are a possibility for why addictions flow from one generation to the next. The environment is easier to look into and study as to why grandparents, parents, and adult children share common qualities of addiction.

It was in the fourth grade when I began my quest for an acting career by taking on leads in plays put on by our music class. I was Buttercup in *HMS Pinafore*. I have a photograph of our cast with hints of tears in my eyes. I sobbed through the rehearsals and Mr. Valentine, the music teacher and director of the play, often had me sit down and asked what was wrong. I always said, "I don't know. I'm just so sad...and scared."

I wanted to be up on stage so badly that I kept doing it anyway. I loved it. I could sing and had stage presence. It was as if there were two distinct sides of me.

Now, putting the pieces of the puzzle together, I remember this was about the time that Grandma Cecelia passed away. Our house took on an atmosphere of hell, with arguing and torrents of violence and fear that progressed to a chronic fevered pitch. The car episode was during this time as well. My tears were a literal crying out for help, but at that time teachers didn't look for signs of students needing help. There weren't therapy services in place like the ones available today.

It was during the childhood of my parents' generation that children began to be considered a bit more important than the animals on the farm, but not much. Now, there are clear signs to look for in children which indicate trouble at home. Back then, children with behavioral problems were considered weird, and, as my mother always said about everyone else except herself, "emotionally unbalanced." Those two words were fed to us throughout our lives and meant a certain and painful end, at least that's what I thought and surmised with each emotion that wasn't a happy one. I often thought I must be going crazy, there's definitely something wrong with me, and I am NOT going to be okay.

The stress and pressure on both my parents was unimaginable with very little money and no one to go to for help since they had burned their bridges with everyone. Through the years, my mother's mental illness and my anxieties and depressions were ignored and denied away. Through the late 60s, into the 70s and 80s as well, the stigma of a person seeking help through a therapist had a moral stigma. That person was deemed "crazy" and unfit. We can now see the dire consequences of what untreated anxiety and depression can inflict on the community and the world. My father's pride wouldn't allow any of us to receive help from outside the family. Interestingly, most people will almost always incorrectly believe that the help they need and the answers for being okay will come from someone in their family. Wouldn't that be great if it were possible?

I later learned through my experiences and my work as well, that most of us were impacted by generations of untreated mental illness, untreated addictions (drugs and alcohol) and unacknowledged, unattended grief. Those of us who grew up during that period of the late 60s, and early 70s, were raised with the rule that "What goes on in this house stays in this house. For that matter, what you think you saw, you didn't see." The general, overall rule was "don't talk about it."

I teetered on the verge of a "mental breakdown" most of my life, especially through my late teen years. I was regarded with suspicion when I showed signs of being nervous or overly needy. In my parents view, one of two things was possible. Either I had done something wrong, or something was very wrong with me. Mom always announced that everyone else was "emotionally unbalanced." She, however, was not. She became the guidepost I used for sanity. If Mom was able to function and made it through certain difficult times in her life, why couldn't I? That phrase, "emotionally unbalanced," stuck with me since it was how I felt most of the time. She would hate it if I went crazy.

During these years, I went through weeks, months and years of fearing another brutal car ride. I began to feel a sense of being beholden to my parents for not killing me, or all of us. It's odd but I experienced such gratitude for living after each Sunday passed. Often the gratitude was shattered, as was the case when one day Mom went into a rage. We were all making too much noise and I could tell she was out of control. I was about ten, the twins were four, and David was three. There was a black look in her eyes as she held in her grasp a butcher block filled with knives. Shielding the kids with my body, I pushed them down the hall and into the last bedroom slamming the door shut behind us. I heard the "ping…ping" of knives hitting the door. I opened the bedroom window and lowered the kids out onto the front lawn; first, the twins so I could lower little David to them. We all made it out and stayed outside until much later when I figured it might be safe to go back inside.

My ability to survive with these people was to dissociate even further than I had ever done before by delving into some book, movie or piece of music. I love the book, *Jane Eyre*, which I read over and over like a meditation, feeling safe within its pages, knowing how the story would end.

However, there were fertile seeds of disgust planted between Mom and me. When I was unable to retreat into my private world and feel okay, I began to act out in ways such as lying, stealing, and cheating as much as possible. Much later in my life, I learned from a therapist that these behaviors were how I nurtured myself. Albeit a sick way, it's all I could come up with to make myself feel better. I started slyly slipping things into my pockets at someone else's house or in a store. I began to act out at school by not listening, not caring, not paying attention but rather talking and passing notes to others. In fourth grade, not long after the car ride, I began to lose the connection I had with my favorite teacher, Mrs. Delany. She had been kind, and she noticed how I struggled, how I often cried with having no answer as to why. She seemed to care whether or not I was okay. She had taken extra time with me during recess, doing what I desperately needed, listening. I had facial tics and odd nervous movements that came and went. My parents would point these odd behaviors out to me with foreboding as if I were showing signs of having something wrong with me.

I became increasingly aware of and worried about the state of my mind. 'Am I going to be okay? Is this what it feels like to go crazy?' My fear was met with Mom's fear when I sought solace from her. When I shared with her how anxious I was feeling or how afraid I was about something or someone, her response was filled with dread. "That doesn't sound good, Debbie. I knew someone who felt that way, and he ended up in a mental institution. That person is emotionally unbalanced." If I continued to be this nervous, I was facing a hopeless, helpless outcome.

In school, I seemed to do well for a short while, and Mrs. Delany would be proud of me. But, ultimately, something would happen, I would act out, and she would look at me, shaking her head with futility. It seemed hopeless. I had someone right there who could help me be okay, but I kept messing up. In looking back on this time, it is clear that for me to have had a therapist to talk to on a regular basis would've been the answer. Instead, we ignored what was going on with me and pretended everything was okay.

This is where Obsessive-Compulsive Disorders kick in with many of us. OCD is an anxiety disorder characterized by recurrent, unwanted thoughts and/or repetitive behaviors.

At home, I became overly concerned about everything. If I could line up the Barbie doll shoes in straight lines, everything would be okay. If I could control my little world, I would be okay. It's when I couldn't find the matching red one for a set of the Barbie shoes that I knew all was lost. In my mind, that made sense to me. Those controlling behaviors begin in that fashion for those of us who see our outside world spin out of control and know there's nothing we can do about it. Would my parents behave so we would be okay? Yes, if I did a certain ritual before school or church. Mine was saying good-bye and acknowledging certain inanimate objects in my bedroom.

Most times, the scenes of the worst arguments took place around the dining room table. We were the audience they enjoyed so much. The small kids cried when they spilled their milk knowing how infuriated Dad got each time it happened. When he walked across the kitchen floor, if he heard sugar crunching under his shoes, he would flip out. We had to scurry and sweep it up. The way Dad reacted would be intolerable in other people's homes; however, it had become quite tolerated and acceptable in ours. I remember being woken up during the middle of the night by my father screaming and hitting someone. I got up quickly and saw him thrashing my brother, David, who was either three or four at the time. David had wet the bed and his crying had woken them up. When I came upon the scene, I heard my brother's arm crack. Dad had broken it. We were told to explain David's broken arm as a fall from a tree.

My father's behavior was a direct result of his childhood and the relationship he had with his father. How else do we learn to behave? Outwardly, I attempted to please them in any way I could while my obsessions with stealing, lying and not caring about myself throughout high school and college grew to a point of almost giving up.

My pattern in relationships with others followed a similar formula. I sought people out who required a great deal of time and energy and were eager to tell me what they thought I had done wrong. Anxiety and depression continued to plague me. When I was in a relationship, I could say I had someone who cared for and loved me. All my relationships had the same element in that the other person's terms took precedence. I never knew whether these men cared about me or not. The way they behaved in our relationships was what they learned from the relationships of their parents or caregivers. I would be okay if my boyfriend, and eventually, my husband ruled the show. All this person had to do was pay attention to me, be somewhat nice, and I concluded he was "the one."

CHAPTER ELEVEN

Real Life Dramas

IN HIGH SCHOOL, I BECAME A CHEERLEADER, BUT I FELT AS THOUGH I didn't belong as a part of the group - always the outsider. I loved drama club and I loved the stage. My first acting experience was as "Chicken Little" in first grade. All the small wooden chairs were lined up against the wall and our classroom was transformed into a stage. I loved the attention and laughter I got as I ran around the room, crying out "The sky is falling! The sky is falling!" Mom wasn't able to attend as the twins had just been born.

In my junior year, the drama director honored me with the 1974 Drama Club award. In front of the school assembly, he stated, "If anyone from Duanesburg Central High School goes to Broadway, it's going to be Debbie Neadle." What an honor! It had been a phenomenal play that year, *The Yankee Doodle Dandy*. I had the female lead and loved every second of it. When the final performance was over, I was sure my parents would finally be so proud of me. I was part of one of the finest groups of performers to come out of that school along with David Seely, Dawn Bartley, Colleen Barton, Phil Bartley,

Gary Dickson, and so many others. Months of rehearsals, preparing and performing was the highlight of my junior year. After our last performance, I went into the crowd in the hall to see what people thought and to be congratulated for the part I played turning out so well. My mom looked at me and said….nothing. I was begging her from my insides to say something kind. Couldn't she say anything? Finally, as my eyes looked into hers beseechingly for something, she said, "I could never do that." I felt like I had flopped. I had no reassurance to trust my instincts that I was good at something. In truth, Mom didn't understand any of what I was doing or who I was becoming. How could she?

It was many years later before I realized that she had been paying me a compliment. Her saying "I could never do that," meant she was aware I had done something that was difficult and beyond her levels of courage and competence. But, at the time, this was way beyond my understanding or maturity level.

I applied to participate in the high school's foreign exchange student program for the summer session of 1974. My mother's attempts to discourage me were in vain. I was finally doing the things I wanted. Wanderlust had always been inside of me, and I loved the idea of being someone important, representing our high school in a foreign country. I sent in an essay for application and got an interview. All the while, both my parents kept saying they would never do that, and asking why I would want to leave even for a short while. I didn't think much about their attitudes then, but now it makes sense that they couldn't understand my desires to be and do something very honorable and good.

I was granted the opportunity of being the 1974 Foreign Exchange student to Mexico City. I left late in June to meet and live with my host family until the end of August. The flight down to Houston was wonderful. I left my confused parents and tearful siblings at the Albany Airport and boarded the plane with the hopes and dreams that everything was going to be okay. I was representing my high school and the United States of America as someone chosen to uphold all the morals and values required of that position. I was on a very noble and honorable journey.

Once on the small plane from Houston to Mexico City, the flight attendant came to me and said someone had offered to buy me a drink. I was now 18, and it was legal, at least it was on this plane flying over international waters down to my host family. I said I'd have a Canadian Club and ginger ale. That's what my father drank every night from his beautiful cut crystal glass which sat in its special place on the end table next to his recliner…within easy reach.

I continued to drink every drink that was offered to me until the plane landed. Of what I can recall, I think I had the most wonderful time. I was feeling better than I had ever felt before. Everyone was paying attention to me. I walked up and down the aisle of the plane talking to everyone as if I were the group leader. I began to realize this was how " happy" felt and this was how it felt to be free. I had finally found the real me.

When the plane landed, all of us poured into the waiting area laughing and causing a scene. Many of the others on the plane were also foreign exchange students meeting up with their host families. My host family stood there waiting for me with what, at one point, may have been smiles and open arms. But, they now had expressions of confusion and concern about this new person, stumbling and laughing, who was to be a part of their family. Damn! I had wanted to make such a good impression.

Was I going to be okay? YES! I had alcohol. The remainder of the three months in Mexico City followed pretty much the same pattern. They had a daughter my age, Marta, and an older son, Andres, who both drank and smoked, too. It was summer and hot in Mexico City. Drinking and smoking menthol cigarettes felt so good! It was also the summer of Nixon's resignation and people constantly asked me what I thought. I knew nothing about it, and I didn't care. In Mexico City, all the young people were politically minded and had at least an opinion about their future and welfare as it pertained to the government. So, I made one up. Drinking and making things up became my way of life.

I couldn't understand why every attempt I made to do well with opportunities I had, I messed up. I started off doing things in a promising way but somehow dropped the ball with myself and gave up. I registered for Spanish classes at the University of Mexico but after a few classes, I ended up partying with friends instead. I loved drinking alcohol because of the way it made me feel.

Looking back, it's as though I remained on a sort of "vacation" allowing alcohol to run and, eventually, ruin so many parts of my life. I never thought drinking was the problem. As the years went by, I drank more often than not. When I felt overwhelmed with responsibility and anxiety, I knew alcohol would be the answer to my being okay.

In recovery, we talk about things we lose if we drink long enough. Some of us begin to lose immediately. Before I left for Mexico, I had one of the sweetest, most loving, kind relationships of my life. Dave and I connected in every way. We were in drama, chorus, everything creative that was available in that very small high school. We vowed to remain true to one another. We even kept our physical relationship sacred until, one day, we would marry. I returned from Mexico in early September, just days before my Senior year began. In Mexico City, I drank my way into the life where I didn't belong. It didn't take long for me to lose interest in Dave, become solely interested in myself and promptly dump him. The one relationship that might have worked out to be the best one for me was the one I gave up.

My Senior year was a bust. The drama coach we all loved had retired the year before. I had few friends, but at least I was filled with my passion for travel and adventure. I thought I would be a flight attendant and travel the world, meeting as many people as I could and making a great impression on all of them. Yet, when it came down to making the decision as to which college I would attend and what I would study, I didn't know what I wanted to do.

What person at that age really knows what they want to do? It's an awful time of confusion and fear of leaving the nest to pursue something someone else may have recommended. There is so much pressure for kids to decide when everyone is asking where you are going to college and what you are going to do with your life.

So, I asked my mother for advice. In high school, she had taken secretarial classes, and high school was as far as she and my father had gone with their educations. That's all she could suggest. In the end, I went for secretarial/administrative studies at a two-year college within the State University of New York (SUNY) system. I hated the studies, but loved the social life!

CHAPTER TWELVE

Wanting To Be That Girl

I HAD NEVER MET AN AFRICAN-AMERICAN PERSON BEFORE, NOR HAD I met anyone who was Jewish, Chinese or Indian. Except for being in Mexico City for three months, I had always spent my life within the community where I grew up. Here at SUNY, Cobleskill, I had the whole melting pot, and I decided to be whoever anyone else thought I should be. That must be the answer in order not to make enemies, I thought. Within a few weeks, I was dating a guy from Long Island, and he was totally controlling. Of course, he was. How would I choose anyone other than that? As far as relationships with men went, I developed a habit of finding the sickest guy in the room and doing whatever he said. How did everyone else know how to be in college and remain themselves? Was I going to be okay in college? Yes, if I drank like everyone else. And, I did.

I even took on a Jewish accent because I thought that might work. By the end of my freshman year in college, yet again, I had stirred up jealousy and controversy. I ended up hanging out with people who felt the same way about themselves as I did about myself. Really crappy.

I couldn't figure out how to "do" life. I meant well, but disaster followed me with the loss of friends on campus. Girls in the dorm began hating me and plotting to make my life hell. This kind of thing had happened in high school, too. Weird!

During the summer break between my first and second year at college, I talked to Mom about why people treated me this way? She said, "Oh, you're just like me. We rub people the wrong way. I think they are all jealous of you." Well then, of course, they were! That was it.

I don't know what I expected to happen in my life. How could I ever be okay when I didn't have a clue what okay was or how to be it? I didn't have an okay role model. I made it up as I went along. I was a pretty good actress, but a really bad script writer.

The first day of my sophomore year in college, I met Geoff as I was standing in line for registration. He had pushed his way in line behind me and acted like he knew a lot of people around us. He paid attention to me by asking if I would hold a poster board for him. His other arm was in a sling, and I did it without even thinking. He was funny and pushy. I liked that. Geoff was wearing an official looking gym sweat suit with an Olympic emblem on it. I was wearing basic, boring bell bottoms and some nameless top. After registration, we walked together for a while, talking. While he did most of the talking, I carried his poster board. The more he paid attention to me, the more I thought this must mean he's "the one."

Geoff was Jewish and had grown up on Eastern Parkway in Brooklyn, New York. He was able to be with people and say things I could never say. We drank a lot, and it seemed like we were having fun. We were inseparable from the beginning. I was going to be okay now that I had found "the one." I was so naive and believed everything he said. He had a gift for telling tales that ended up to be mostly lies. As it turned out, he hadn't done the things on an Olympic team that he claimed he had. There were trophies from races he had won and deer heads in his dorm room from his hunting expeditions. Later, it was all proven to be lies, but at the time, I believed all of it and fell in love. At least, I fell into what I thought was love.

Within a few months of dating, we went to a Halloween party at a fraternity house off campus. Although he wasn't in it, Geoff knew most of the guys. We arrived together and drank a lot from the start. Like most of us who need help being comfortable in social situations, drinking helped make that part much easier. I became more animated and started talking with some people from the frat house. After a while, I realized Geoff was nowhere to be found. One of our friends, Steve, came up to me as I wandered around alone and asked me what happened with Geoff and me because he had seen Geoff leave with another girl. Steve took me home in my drunken, confused state and helped me to my dorm room. My roommate was there and helped settle me down. Steve left saying he was sorry things turned out the way they did. He asked me if we could get together sometime, but I was rude and said, "No way." Why would I? He was too nice and I was humiliated.

The next day, my stomach and head were a mess. I couldn't believe my relationship with Geoff was over, and I had believed he was who he said he was. Later in the day, he came to my room and asked if we could talk. He went on and on about what a terrible person he was. He had a problem, he told me, when he drank and did things he shouldn't do. He needed help. He said he was weak and needed me to help him become a better man. With a vow he would never leave me again for someone else, we went on for three more years. Ever present for the underdog, I stuck by him even when he was at his lowest.

The following semester, it became public knowledge that his claims of participation in the Olympic Games and the Olympic jersey he wore both years of college were lies. He had given speeches on campus of his experiences and led people to believe he was part of the cycling team.

Through a friend, I found out about the lies, so I went to Geoff's dorm room to confront him and find out if it was true. He was lying on his bed refusing to look at me and told me to go away. As I was leaving the dorm, one of our friends, Mike, caught up with me and told me it was true. Geoff had lied about all of it. One of the professors had checked on Geoff's story because to him it had all sounded suspicious. Even though Geoff had gone to such lengths to deceive all of us, I went back to the dorm and insisted he talk to me. I told him I would stand by him even if everyone hated him. Of course, I did.

We both graduated in May of 1977 and I decided I wanted to move to New York City to be an actress and a dancer. During college breaks, we had gone down to Geoff's mother's beautiful apartment in Manhattan where she now lived. I wanted our life together to be where he was from and where I wanted my career to begin. I had watched *That*

Girl with Marlo Thomas for years while growing up, and I thought I knew exactly how to do this. My ability to feign the "life" of television was masterful. The television show aired from the late 60s and into the 70s. Marlo Thomas played a young woman, Ann, who went to live in New York City with her goal to be an actress. Ann was my guide. Each week, she would show me how it was done by getting various kinds of jobs, going on auditions and, of course, having this wonderful boyfriend, Don. She also had great parents who always came to her rescue. She would get into various kinds of trouble but manage to rise above all of it and, eventually, get what she wanted.

I thought this was turning out perfectly. I had Geoff. We would get settled into his brother's vacant apartment in Brooklyn Heights that summer of 1977 and we could start our lives together. However, on the ride down from Delanson to Brooklyn, Geoff told me he was starting Boston University in the fall. I was in shock. He would be staying in Brooklyn for the summer only. He told me his mother was making him do this. He didn't want to leave me, but he had to. There seemed to be a pattern of behavior where he would drop these bombs, and I wouldn't say much at all. I would go with the flow, tolerating the intolerable for much longer than I should. I had no idea how to stand up for myself or question what his motives were. I don't remember him hanging out with me much that summer. I was lucky that his brother, Mark, was doing an internship somewhere outside of the city so I could stay a couple of months until I got on my feet.

By the end of that first summer in New York City, I had found a third-floor walkup studio apartment on Henry Street in Brooklyn Heights, and Geoff was off to Boston. The apartment had one huge room with a small bathroom off to the side. I had a blow-up mattress for a few months. It was exciting in the beginning, even though I had only one closet for clothes and another closet that had been made into the kitchen. There was a two burner stove and small fridge... all I needed. I washed dishes in the bathroom and thought it was all very "Marlo Thomas like." For me, living on Henry Street was a sign. In *Funny Girl*, Barbara Streisand played Fanny Brice, who had grown up on Henry Street. I knew all of the songs. Once I could afford it, I bought a pull out sofa to sleep on. So far, so good.

Not long after I arrived in New York City, I found a job as a secretary at an advertising agency. The ad agency where I worked was on lower Broadway around the corner from the World Trade Center. The North and South towers had recently been completed. I worked during the week 9 a.m. to 5 p.m. On the weekends, I began taking acting and dancing classes at Carnegie Hall. I loved it all until I didn't love it at all. It was a scary time for me as it was all so unfamiliar. The living conditions were seedy and as deplorable as depicted in the movie, *Taxi Driver*. It was the summer of the Son of Sam, a serial killer who murdered six people and created chaos in New York City. Everyone else seemed to know how to "do" life. I didn't. No matter how hard I tried, I was unable to deal with being overwhelmed, alone and lonely.

Unlike the parents in *That Girl*, my parents never came to see me. They lived only a three-hour train ride away, but they didn't like the city and couldn't bring themselves to visit even once. This was the part of Marlo Thomas' life in *That Girl* which didn't come anywhere close to mine. She had parents who called or drove down to check in on her from time to time. My parents hadn't wanted me to do any of this. In fact, on the day I left Delanson with Geoff to drive to New York City, my mom had a panic attack and my father turned his head away from me as I attempted to give him a kiss goodbye. That was my fond farewell. They couldn't create a different, better life for themselves and, therefore, didn't know how to support me in trying to make a better life for myself. I didn't understand that at the time.

My youngest sister, Dina, was traumatized that I was leaving her. She was used to me being there for her, especially when things were truly bad with my parents. The twins and David all had each other. Their lives were getting busy in high school, and twins always had that way of living in their shared private world. They would be okay. I worried about Dina and felt guilty leaving her, but I knew I had to, at least, try New York.

I may not have been a working actress, but I was diligently working at acting out my badly written life script. For the first year, I spent many weekends taking the train to Boston to visit Geoff. He rarely came back to New York anymore citing multiple commitments that kept him there. He only made the trip if he needed something from his mother but I faithfully took the train up to Boston College so we could be together. On other weekends, I used the little money I had to take acting and dancing lessons. I loved the lifestyle of the actors and dancers. We came and went with crazy clothes and intense looks of having somewhere very important to go. I never felt fearful when I was with theater people. It was the era of *A Chorus Line*. I had an improv class with a Broadway director who gave us tickets to many of the shows. I loved *Chorus Line*; clearly a show made for me.

Sundays were the worst days for me when I was in the city alone. It seemed everyone had their families or friends with whom they spent time. Often, I'd take the subway from Brooklyn Heights into Manhattan and wander around Rockefeller Center window shopping. I felt like a fish out of water being there on my own. I could've gone to more classes, but I didn't have the extra money, so I spent time sitting in St. Patrick's Cathedral watching people. Although I sometimes sat through a mass, it felt very foreign to me. We had gone to church every Sunday growing up but since college I had stopped doing that.

My apartment was close to a Russian Orthodox Catholic Church, which was dark and strangely elaborate inside. I went to mass there once, but I didn't like it. I preferred sitting in St. Patrick's on Sundays with its stunningly beautiful interior. I could go into my fantasy world there and I didn't have to try to fit in. Eventually, I became relaxed when the weekend came. I knew St. Patrick's was there and I was still okay.

{ ✈ }

CHAPTER THIRTEEN

My New York State of Mind

LEADING UP TO THE SPRING OF 1979, CRIME IN THE SUBWAYS OF NEW York City became legendary as people were randomly pushed off the platforms into the path of oncoming subway trains. A vigilante group called The Guardian Angels formed in February, 1979, took it into their own hands to patrol the subways to keep them safe. This created a chronic state of fear and confusion for passengers of the subways as to what the city was doing to keep us all safe.

I had my first full-blown panic attack while riding on the subway on a Sunday morning. I was severely hung over from a night of heavy drinking at a party given by some theater people I hardly knew. That party was somewhere out in Queens so I really had no idea where I was. There were a few people I knew from my improv class at the party, but once I started drinking, everyone became my friend.

The more I drank at this party, the more my "funny self " transformed into me crying about Geoff to anyone who would listen. He must still love me. He said he did, but it seemed strangely similar to what happened in college. Was he planning on finding someone else? Had he already? I wasn't the best judge of how other people felt about me. I was living in my head where the story I was creating was going really well.

I must've been a sloppy bother to those people at the party. That's what happened when I drank too much and that made me even more depressed. How did other people know how to drink and not get like this? They were able to talk normally and look grown-up doing it. This whole New York thing didn't turn out like I thought it would.

At this party, I was huddled with a group of people sitting on the floor sharing cheap wine and stories of failed auditions. I slept on the floor that night with most of the others who kept drinking into the wee hours. It was late by the time the party ended, and I was too drunk to go home to Brooklyn Heights by myself. I woke up that Sunday morning feeling horrible. I could barely lift my head and I needed water! I couldn't imagine making my way back to Brooklyn by myself as I didn't like being "by myself" any more.

I made my way to the subway hoping the trip back to Brooklyn Heights would be quick and painless. It was so hot outside, making me feel worse. I was somewhere far out in Queens, so it wasn't an easy route back to my apartment. I sat in the back of one of the nearly empty cars on the train. As the old subway car banged back and forth, screeching its way against the walls and careening down the black, dark tunnels, I held on tight. Suddenly, I felt my heart begin to race and the entire train seemed out of control. The lights inside the train kept going on and off and I felt like I was going to die. I looked up to see if anyone else was as alarmed as I was that something bad was happening to us. People looked odd to me and seemed to stare at me as if I were the one with something wrong. I felt myself going insane right in that disgusting subway train.

I stood up in a full-blown panic attack, screaming inside my head that I had to get out of there. Lights were swirling around me. I couldn't breathe well. This train was not stopping! I had to get off immediately! I didn't say any of this out loud, but inside my hungover, terrified head, I begged for the subway train to stop screeching, stop moving…I had to get out!

Finally, the train began to slow down, and I raced for the door with my eyes open wide in as much panic as if I were running from people who were wanting to push me onto the tracks. The danger from which I was running was in my head. I believed I was going crazy. There I was on my own, out of the train and running madly up those steep stairs into the morning air. Was I going to be okay? Probably not! I needed fresh air.

Once out of the subway, standing on the sidewalk, I looked around at where I had gotten off of the subway and I didn't see anything that looked familiar. Where was I? I needed help. I needed a hospital, but I wouldn't get back onto the subway again. I could never go back down there. I was starting to breathe a bit better, but it was so hot. This city had no fresh air! I wandered around looking for a street sign that might help me, but when I found one, it didn't help. I was in a panic attack fog. I felt drunk but not in a good way. Finally, I decided the only way to get back to my apartment was to take a taxi that I certainly couldn't afford but I did it anyway.

What a relief it was to be in my apartment. I felt much better. I drank a ton of water and then, I called Geoff. I kept telling him how much I missed him and how afraid I was here in New York City by myself. I wanted to move to Boston – that very next week!

He didn't seem as excited about it as I was. It would soon be the beginning of the fall term. He had stayed in Boston during the summer to do an internship for his major which was communications. Once I was off the phone with him, I couldn't seem to settle myself. Here I was again… overwhelmed, unsupported and abandoned when I needed him the most. This couldn't be happening. I had to go to work the next day and I wasn't getting on that subway ever again. I tried taking the bus to work the next morning and was over an hour late. I had no idea about the bus systems and chose one that had a stop close to my office. I reluctantly went back to the subway each day that week and barely made it through without having another full-blown panic attack. I made up my mind I was going to Boston the next Friday after work and, hopefully, get our relationship back on track.

Just knowing I was going to see Geoff again made it easier for me to get on the subway, especially the closer Friday came. I was so relieved and excited to be on my way to Boston that Friday night that I drank more than I normally did on the train. Once I got to Boston, Geoff was there at the station, and beside him, stood a girl I didn't know. I ran up and hugged him. It felt so good. He introduced this girl, Valerie, as a friend. I didn't pay much attention as I was drunk and had too much to tell him and complain about. I felt so much better with him. I was going to be okay.

We got to Geoff's dorm where Valerie, Geoff and I sat in the lounge. I wasn't picking up on the fact that Geoff was acting distant and that the two of them sat close together on the lounge sofa. Then, came the bomb. Geoff announced that he and Valerie were a couple. I hazily remember hearing what they were saying, but not getting it. Couldn't he have told me this before I made this trip up to Boston? I was very passive in my devastation. I started crying but not doing much else…not screaming or throwing things. I was a very sad drunk.

I was in such disbelief. This was not how the Marlo Thomas *That Girl* episode ended. She got the boyfriend who stayed with her through every hardship she endured. Geoff was not following the television script. He was behaving like himself. He had done this before, and I was hoping he had changed. Had he done anything to change? Not really. I thought things were going according to plan, but he had been dating Valerie from the first few days at Boston University.

They asked me if I wanted to stay overnight and leave in the morning. I didn't. They took me back to the train station where they both helped me get the ticket and board the train. I had little to no reaction. I couldn't do anything except sit still and take their help. Looking back, it seemed totally unacceptable behavior on his part to do something like that to me…or to anyone. All I wanted was to get out of that city and away from them. Hadn't I wanted to get out of New York City to be in Boston? I was ill-equipped with any language or any fury to release on them. I hadn't ever stood up for myself before. How would I know how to do that now? Since I was never allowed to disagree with anyone while growing up, or at least in adolescence, where would I get the words or courage to do it now?

I don't remember much about the train ride back except that I drank the entire five hours. I spent the last few dollars I had for a taxi to my apartment. I was alone, on my own, unsupported, overwhelmed and abandoned...again. This trip was a push toward a speedy spiral into insanity.

> How we were treated as children is the guide we use in later years as to how we allow others to treat us. We may not see it in the beginning of our relationships, yet further down the road, and after a few "red flags," we will recognize the way a person is treating us as eerily familiar. Many people, men and women, return to abusive situations, not because there is something wrong with them or they are asking for more, but because this situation is familiar in the deepest of ways. Until we recognize the need for change and make it, many of us return to what's familiar even when it's sick and bad for us and in some instances, until it kills us.

It became increasingly more and more difficult to do the simplest things. I couldn't go into grocery stores, movie theaters or even crowded restaurants without fear of losing control. I feared a part of me would take over and send me into the oblivion of a mental institution.

I didn't know then that the answer was not "control," but, instead, to let go, feel my emotions, and reach out for help from others.

I began to miss work. I no longer went to acting or dancing classes. I became isolated in my studio apartment that I could no longer afford. Finally, just before Christmas of that year, I called my parents asking if I could come home. Mom answered the phone and said, "Sure, you can come home," although her tone sounded as though she was less than happy about it.

Dad finally came to the city. It was the only time either one of my parents ever came. He and my cousin, Georgie, came to get me and take me home. Both Dad and Georgie were so terrified to be in Brooklyn that it took them less than an hour to pack my things into Georgie's truck. Dad said, "Let's get the hell out of here." After almost two years of being in New York City attempting to live my dreams, I felt both relieved and defeated as we drove back to Delanson, mostly in silence.

What I know now but didn't know then was how the combination of feeling overwhelmed, highly stressed, without support and abandoned led me down the path of anxiety-induced depression. I tried again and again through the years to be a strong, responsible member of society and start my life over. However, just when I thought my life was going well, I would get blindsided by something else.

My relief in returning home turned to defeat soon after my first day back. In fact, the very next day as I helped Mom set the table, she informed me, "I knew you couldn't do it." My mother's way with words was like a punch to my solar plexus. It took me a very long time to recover from that one. I was filled with shame at the prospect of not having a job or boyfriend at this ripe old age of 22 and having to start all over from square one. From how she did life, Mom could not comprehend anything I had done or was now thinking of doing with my life.

The loss of my dream of acting in New York City brought about a deep, profound grief and it seemed as if it would go on and on for the rest of my life. The early twenties are a time to explore, enjoy and try different things without putting the tag of "mistake" on every endeavor that didn't work out. I didn't know that then. A few days after I returned to my parent's home in Delanson, I realized I was impulsive in leaving New York City. I felt I should return to try again, with or without Geoff, who, by the way, had begun calling me, imploring me to see him again. My pattern of accepting unacceptable behavior and still loving the idea of attention almost had me wanting to try being with him again. Maybe now, I would be okay if Geoff and I had a fresh start. We began to talk on a regular basis, mostly about him and his plans for when he graduated from Boston University. As far as my plans.....I had none. Would I be okay if we tried again?

CHAPTER FOURTEEN

Chasing Love and Choosing Poorly

WHEN I RETURNED HOME FROM NEW YORK CITY, I SPOKE WITH MY neighbors, Steve and Bev, who had a ceramic tile, marble, and granite distributorship, about a job with their company. I had often babysat their daughter when I was in high school. We agreed that I would start working at their business, Best Tile, as a sales representative. I was to work inside the showrooms and outside at flooring dealerships and calling on architects within the tri-state area of New York, Vermont, and western Massachusetts. It was a beginning into the next chapter of my life.

I began to enjoy working at Best Tile where on some days I would dress up and assist customers in selecting tile for their new homes. Other days, I would wear jeans, t-shirts and steel-toed boots to drive a fork-lift, unload tractor trailers and lift heavy boxes of tile, working alongside funny, crazy, dirty men in the warehouse. I had a new-found love in this world of rough, tough men who worked hard and played hard. It seemed so much like what my father had done as a crane operator on the barges on the Mohawk River when he worked on the locks and dams of what was the former Erie Canal system.

At my place of work, it was about contractors, tile setters and truck drivers. I went from the showroom to the warehouse throughout the day, lifting heavy tile boxes and accepting that this was the life for me. There was dirt, grunge and, eventually, after the store closed, lots of drinking. I was one of the guys and, finally, I felt I belonged somewhere. Steve and Bev rarely stayed around for the after work drink fests. The guys and I had a blast.

The manager of Best Tile in Colonie, New York, was a man named Chet. He was Italian, thin and wiry and reminded me of how Frank Sinatra looked in his much younger years. Chet was a tough boss and showed no favorites. There had never been a woman working at the store before, at least not in the capacity of doing what the guys did, so it was awkward at first between the two of us. Chet had a fantastic sense of humor, mostly at the expense of others, but still it made the days fly by. He taught me how to drive a forklift, how to lift boxes without hurting my back and, eventually, we stayed unloading tractor trailers that arrived late in the evening. I loved it and I developed a crush on him.

We drank beer while we waited for trucks to come in and began this very strange relationship based only on and as a direct result of alcohol and late nights at the store. Chet was not interested in having a steady relationship, so that made me want him all the more. I was spiraling down into a world of drinking and working where nothing else really mattered.

I loved the idea of continuing my education, so in the fall of 1981, after living with my parents for almost a year, I entered SUNY, Albany. I hoped to obtain my BA in International Business and Languages. I also moved into an apartment with my friend, Laura. I felt as if I were beginning my life again and that now everything would be okay. I loved being out on my own. My drinking calmed down a bit as I began focusing on my studies. I was less interested in partying with the people at Best Tile and more interested in possibly becoming a better person. One of the best opportunities that came out of being enrolled at SUNY, Albany was my ability to seek counseling which was included in my tuition. For the first time, I was able to see that therapy was not something to fear or even do only when someone is at the end of his or her rope. I began working with a therapist learning there was nothing wrong with going to therapy. In fact, there was something very right about what I was finding out about myself and what was not acceptable about how I had been treated growing up.

In 1984, Chet was asked to be a partner in the next Best Tile location to be developed which was in Wexford and Cranberry Township, just outside of Pittsburgh, Pennsylvania. We still hung out together, but I wasn't interested in moving there if we were not going to be committed to one another. I had completed my BA at SUNY, Albany the year before with plans to move to Europe somewhere and teach English as a second language. I still had the urge to travel which had begun with my trip to Mexico City. Pittsburgh had no appeal to me, at all. After the long suffering relationship I had with Geoff, I was hesitant to be involved with someone else, living life on his terms. I wanted to live life on my terms. I didn't want to lose what Chet and I had together even if our connection still was mostly work and drinking related. In 1985, I moved to Wexford, Pennsylvania, and joined Chet working alongside him.

I, once again, made a big life decision without much planning. That was a pattern I followed for many years to come. I thought when I made big changes in my life, the answer to "Am I Going to Be Okay?" would be positive.

Chet and I were amazing business partners, working with customers, and designing displays; however, he wasn't interested in the same future goals of marriage and children as I was. Fear kept me in a situation that showed everyone around us, except me, that it would be best if I left Chet. Hindsight tends to be clearer than in the moment. I probably would've been okay on my own; however, I was strangely attached to this man who wasn't nearly as interested in me as I was in him.

I convinced Chet that we should get married. He was a very reluctant husband and a reluctant father. Of course, he was! Marriage and kids weren't what he had planned for his life. He wanted to work hard to establish the business and use any free time to hunt and drink with his buddies. I thought if I got married, then I would be okay; when we had children, then I would be okay; when we were married for ten years, then I would be okay.

I continued to use these time frames as benchmarks of success for staying sane. Eventually, we designed a massive home for ourselves and styled it using ideas from the photos I took while on our many business trips to Italy and Spain. Of course, with each of these big life happenings, I became more overwhelmed, unsupported and felt utterly abandoned.

One of the lasting effects of being raised in emotional, verbal and physical abuse (with occasional moments of humor, kisses and hugs) is we find those familiar traits in others. Then we befriend them, chase them, marry them, and continue the approval dance with whoever fits the bill. I was not interested in the very nice, stable dentist I dated while working at Best Tile in Colonie. I was desperate for Chet, who was my boss. He was cold, disgruntled and not happy with me working there. Is it true that we marry someone who treats us in the manner that is familiar to us even though it's sick and bad for us? In my case, yes, it was true. How would I know not to be attracted to that? It was an exhausting relationship with Chet. From its alcohol-soaked beginnings until the end of our marriage, I knew nothing of how to do this very grown up life.

How would I know how to maintain a healthy relationship? How does anyone? We learn by watching what we have witnessed in our early lives and even after that. That is pretty much the guide to being wives and mothers. For me, I remained in the world of books, television and movies to find how to do it. Being pretty, thin, dynamic and bulldozer-like was the answer for me. If people were not interested in me, I would "take them hostage," as it is phrased in the rooms of recovery; doing them a favor, so to speak.

It was hell as I went through my twenties and early thirties trying to do what I thought I was supposed to do with people who may or may not have been interested but went along anyway. The pit of my stomach was always clenched tight as were my jaws and teeth. I was so clenched during the move to Pittsburgh in 1985 that my jaw eventually locked shut. I was able to open it just a slight bit but eventually had an operation on one side of my jaw. This condition was called Temporal Mandibular Joint Dysfunction (TMJ), a syndrome where the eventual clenching and grinding brought me to a point of keeping my mouth shut. How interesting!

Was I pretending to "do" life as it should be done? Is this why we marry, have kids and fill those years with chaos and come out the other side yearning for something else, someone else, someplace else? Why did we marry this person in the first place? Lost, alone and lonely still, even after all the things that were supposed to give meaning to our lives.

CHAPTER FIFTEEN

Wife, Mother, and Teetering on the Brink

OUR SON, CHET (CHETTY), WAS BORN IN 1988 AND DAUGHTER, Katherine, was born in 1991. I believed being married and having children would be the solution to overcoming all my fears. What evolved was the life of a single mother who happened to be married. Each big life decision that I persistently suggested Chet and I do, only made us distant from one another. I came in and out of episodes of depression when the children were very small while Chet became focused mostly on the business, leaving home early in the morning and not coming home until very late at night.

I remember very little of the nine months before either our son or daughter was born. The summer before Chetty was born was the hottest on record and my husband, Chet, got us an air conditioner for the living room. That was the most caring, loving thing he had ever done for me. My hormones were aligned with the moon and the stars when I was pregnant, so for the first time in my female, hormonal life, I was calm, peaceful and horny as hell. In those respects, nine months went rather quickly.

The years following my move to the Pittsburgh area didn't bring Mom and me closer together at all. She wanted to be more a part of my life, but I didn't want her there. When my first baby was born, I told her not to come down. I wanted it to be just Chet, the new baby and me. None of the relatives came.

When it came time for an important event in the lives of our children, both sides of the family came or no one did. There was jealousy and hell to pay if things weren't totally equal — more so with Chet's family than mine, although his father had moved in and lived with us most of the time we were married. It created enormous stress trying to keep everyone happy.

Nothing, not books or other people's advice and experiences, prepared me for what lie ahead in motherhood. I loved being a first-time mother and those first few years with the baby were pretty good although I would not see those libido-soaked days again until my next pregnancy with Katherine. Baby Chetty and I were inseparable. I thought of how similar this was to how things were with Mom and me before the other kids came along. I set myself up for the confusion and disconnection of my true self at that time by trying to be the exact opposite of my mother in every way. How I was truly feeling about being a mother never came into play. Who I needed to be was made up in my head, but the baby and I did our thing, which probably ended up being more like Mom and me than I thought. Not until years later, when Katherine announced to me that I was like Mom, did that realization settle in.

Rather than calming my inner turmoil, being a wife and mother 24/7 brought me to episodes of deep anxiety and depression where I seemed to teeter, yet again, on the brink of insanity. I began seeing therapists in Pittsburgh while I binged on alcohol through my thirties and forties. I didn't think alcohol had much of an impact on how I was feeling emotionally, mentally and physically. I was wrong. It was impacting all aspects of my life since alcohol is a depressant. Whatever depression medication I was prescribed lost its effect as I drank more and more often.

During my second pregnancy, Luisa came into our lives. She was a wonderful woman in her mid-50s when we met. She was dating a friend of ours and when we joined them for dinner, I liked her immediately. Born and raised in Madrid, Luisa had married an American GI back in 1967 and moved to Pittsburgh shortly after they married. When we met, Luisa had just gone into remission from breast cancer. She had recently gone through a devastating divorce after finding out her husband was having an affair with his secretary.

Soon after meeting her, Chet and I asked if she would help me a couple of days a week. Chetty was a baby, and I was pregnant with Katherine. Luisa became one of the family as she was at our house most every day. She served as a grandmother figure for Chetty and Katherine, calling him her "sunshine" and Katherine her "princessita." In addition, she was a beloved helpmate and companion for me. She was a mediator between Chet and myself and filled in when he was not around. My son and I had been extremely attached since his birth. When Katherine was born and Luisa came into our lives, Katherine became extremely attached to Luisa. Chetty hated them both. He must have felt as abandoned as I did when my siblings were born.

Not long after Katherine was born, I started to feel overwhelmed and began thinking that having two children was like having ten. Even with Luisa's help, my mental and emotional stability eroded quickly. I began to see a therapist regularly, who insisted I didn't need medication. However, I believed I needed it desperately and sought help from a psychiatrist and a new therapist.

> Every human being has anxiety, unless we are robots. Mental illness doesn't equate to crazy or weak. Our ancestors suffered greatly without the relief we have today through medication and the ability to talk about what is going on within us. What was given the label "nervous breakdown" previously, we now realize is chronic, high anxiety without relief – untreated mental illness.

I dreaded each major holiday with the children, especially Christmas. There was a horrible dread each year as it loomed near. Right after we cleared the Thanksgiving dishes, I felt the immense responsibility to remain sane so that I would not be put into a mental institution before Christmas morning. It pounded my inner world without mercy. All I could think was these two poor innocent children had me as a mother, and I was failing miserably. The notion was probably not true in most areas, somewhat true in others.

Sometimes, mothers keep secret how we truly feel about being mothers. "Am I Going to Be Okay? There's a little one crying for something and I'm so overwhelmed, I can't pour milk this morning." Waves of sadness, coated with fear, settled in and haunted me through this season of love, light, and happiness. I scouted everywhere for the right presents, food, and holiday spirit to shower all over everyone while I felt despair. There was a constant running inner dialog that kept me from falling over the edge of mental illness, certain destitute aloneness, and eventual death. I sometimes still go to those places without knowing why I'm feeling that way. I imagined my children would have an image of me in a cold, lonely mental hospital bed with a fake tree in the lobby. That image kept me on my toes in case I ever got the notion to let up on myself.

I loved being a mother, and yet, there were mornings, such as those during festive times, when I couldn't imagine one more day of taking care of anyone else, even the cat…especially the cat.

The kids and I became so attached to Luisa that even the thought of her leaving at night brought terrible anxiety. I felt alone, unsupported and abandoned when she wasn't with me. When Chetty was seven and Katherine was four, Luisa told us she was going to take a trip back to Madrid, Spain, to see her relatives for a month. I was petrified that I couldn't make it without her. Soon after Luisa left for Madrid, the kids and I flew to meet her there.

Luisa was with us for eight years before she passed away. Her cancer returned when she was 58. She remained caring for us until she was unable to do so. She loved us and we loved her with all our hearts. The week before Luisa passed away on April 22, 1998, we all went to see her in the hospital and Chetty reached up to her and gave her his "blankie."

> The most powerful impact on a human being is the initial loss of a loved one through death or loss of a relationship. Anxiety begins there, "Am I going to be okay?" has one of its first major challenges here. If the person, place or thing is the only person, place, or thing to sooth and comfort us through the pain of loss, then anxiety steps in to answer "probably not."

I couldn't imagine life without her. I was anchorless without Luisa to care for and about me. The loss of Luisa impacted our family with immeasurable grief. We continue to have tender loving memories of this wonderful person who brought love and laughter into our anxiety riddled lives.

Mr. Rodgers, who developed "Mr. Rodger's Neighborhood" in Pittsburgh, Pennsylvania, established a program for grieving children called "The Caring Place." Children have the opportunity to begin to heal from their losses by sharing with others in their age group through activities and talking. I took Chetty and Katherine to weekly sessions there in order for them to work through the beginning stages of their grief. The Caring Place also supported parents and loved ones. Our group was facilitated by a woman who encouraged us to share our stories. Finally, I had a place to share about the loss of Luisa, which opened the door to share all the grief that had accumulated within me.

I continued to seek therapy, take medicine and even began a meditation practice attempting to heal from the loss of Luisa. Progressively, as the kids became older and moved into activities of their own, I escaped into drinking. I felt I was doing the parenting thing on my own, and I was. Chet became even more detached and our arguments became intolerable for the kids. They begged us to stop fighting. I tried every type of anti-depressant on the market, but nothing was helping me. When I finally admitted the truth to my psychiatrist that I was a heavy drinker, she realized I wasn't falling down a dark hole into insanity. My anxiety was a direct result of my alcohol consumption.

My grief over Luisa's death propelled me into a phase of life and drinking that no one could imagine, especially me.

CHAPTER SIXTEEN

The World Comes Unglued

ON SEPTEMBER 11, 2001, I WAS IN THE MARSHALL ELEMENTARY SCHOOL in Wexford, Pennsylvania, helping out in the library. I did this every Tuesday from 7:30 a.m. until about 11:00 a.m. My friend, Christine McDonald, and I were putting books away and catching up on some of the details of our lives. My daughter, Katherine, was in fourth grade and Christine's daughter, Kelsey, was in fifth. At about 9:25 a.m., someone from the principal's office walked calmly into the library, went over to the head librarian, took her aside and quietly told her that a plane had hit the World Trade Center. The librarian informed us of this, and told us not to make any changes in our demeanor. She instructed us not to say anything to the children or each other, but when we could get away, go into the front office where the television was on, and we could see what was happening.

Right about then, Katherine's class filed in and sat at the smaller desks, two lines of them facing each other. I could feel a tingling of heightened awareness which happens when on alert. That seemed to solidify my memory of the beginning of the hell of 9/11. Each of us has a memory of where we were and what we were doing on this day. All of the teachers in that school and in the North Allegheny School District were alerted by email and told to remain perfectly calm, say nothing, and go about their day until further notice.

Christine went to the office first and came back more pale than when she left. "Another plane hit the other tower," she said. "They are commercial planes and they hit the towers on purpose."

Leaving to see what was happening, I had a surreal sense that each of us was on our own to save ourselves and families, yet totally united in the common goal of hope and prayer. Gathered around the small television, others from the office were watching in horror as Tom Brokaw and Katie Couric managed to report and react as best they could.

Back in the library, Christine and I assisted the librarian as we always did, either with the children or keeping the books in order where they belonged. It felt like meaningless work right then.

Within 30 minutes, another woman from the front office came in and took the librarian and the rest of us into a side office. She told us that another plane had gone into the Pentagon, another one went down in Somerset, and it is believed Pittsburgh is also a target.

I looked at Christine and said, "I feel as if this is the beginning of the end of the world. I always wondered if I would be alive when it happened." I had wondered, off and on throughout my life, whether the world would blow up in a nuclear holocaust or something as drastic. It seemed it could be a distinct possibility now.

It was quietly but quickly announced that the school was on lockdown. No one was to be let in or out of the building. This information was sent district wide by email to all schools in South Western Pennsylvania. The lockdown didn't last long because parents began coming to the schools to pick up their children. The library was located next to the lobby, and hearing the banging on the huge glass doors was unavoidable. Parents wouldn't leave and demanded their children.

Eventually, as calmly as possible, the parents were allowed inside the lobby and highly encouraged to leave their children in school as it is one of the safest, most secure buildings in the area. None of them listened. Students in grades kindergarten through third were told only that their moms were here to take them home and they had the rest of the day off.

Kids came down the hall towards the lobby, totally unaware of what was going on, happy and ready to have a day off. The mothers were the ones who were crying and instilled fear and worry in all of us.

Quickly, those of us working near the lobby were to clear it as best we could, and if we wanted to take our children home, that was up to us. I made the decision that both Katherine and Chetty were probably better off remaining in school. The Marshall Middle School where Chetty was in the seventh grade was across the parking lot from the

Elementary School where Katherine attended. From what I heard, the teachers had told the 4th and 5th graders what had happened in a general way. In 6th, 7th, and 8th grades, they had the television on. Chetty later said he was glad he was with his class and stayed in school. They were encouraged to remain calm; to leave would've started a whole new panic.

I left the Marshall Elementary School and went straight to our Catholic church, not far from the school. Saints John and Paul was a relatively new church combining three areas of our northern Pittsburgh suburbs. The church was packed, and the common bond of being a refuge of community and prayer was something I have never experienced before or since. Many of us knew each other from the births of our children, church activities, and school. Hundreds of us said prayers together and sang songs being led by someone up front. The spirit did, indeed, move us.

Before I left the school, my brother, Dave, called me from California to make sure I was okay. Once the news had broken that Flight 93 had gone down close to Pittsburgh, each of my siblings called to find out if we were safe. All five of us always wanted to know we were all okay. Dave and his wife, Tammy, out in Pleasanton, California were all right. The twins and Dina were fine, as well.

No one had heard from Mom or Dad. My sisters and brother were so angry with them that they hadn't called any of us, as the plane had gone down so close by. Dave called Mom and Dad and yelled at them,

I think for the first time ever, for not thinking to call me or any of us to see if we were okay.

Later on that day, Mom called and asked how we were. They were in Maine on their anniversary trip and hadn't thought they needed to call. They figured we were okay, or if not, we would have called them. Who does that? They were an island unto themselves and always had been, always would be.

CHAPTER SEVENTEEN

Facing the Truth

ON MARCH 24, 2004, I BEGAN MY JOURNEY INTO THE LAND OF THE living by ending my daily obsession with alcohol. I was 46 when I got sober. I didn't stop drinking because I drove drunk a lot of the time, which I did. Nor did I get sober because of driving drunk in a blackout where I nearly killed my kids and their friends. It wasn't even because it was ruining my relationships with everyone around me. I stopped drinking because, after years of trying multiple antidepressants, my psychiatrist told me that she was going to have to look at the diagnosis of Bipolar Disorder.

This scared me into telling her the truth of my drinking. My anxieties throughout my life had proven to me that I couldn't "do" real life. Most days I felt as though I was going crazy. As a child, I had cried often. In school and at home, I was shamed and reprimanded for it. Crying in school and church became such a problem that Mom even suggested to Dad that I might need to see someone for help. Dad wouldn't allow it. He said I must stop being so sensitive. I began a series of facial tics that would slowly subside as I started a new one.

I blinked and opened my eyes wide as if in shock, then twitched my nose or jerked my head from shoulder to shoulder like a windshield wiper. Once I had no new nervous actions to take, I would repeat. The not so subtle message I received from my parents was that if I didn't stop doing these strange things, they wouldn't know what to do with me. It was clear to me that I was doomed to live out my life in a mental institution, probably sooner rather than later, and no one would ever see me again.

As an adult, I sought help on my own and had found Dr. Elizabeth Hepler-Smith, who was now my psychiatrist. She had been very diligent with my care for about five years when I finally began my journey to sobriety. Alcohol had worked for a long time to calm my inner turmoil. As my anxieties increased over the mounting responsibilities of a failing marriage and two troubled teens, I relied heavily on what alcohol was giving me. Sometimes, I felt I was closer to God when I drank. I could find that place of peace within to pray, but that place had long gone to blackout drinking and belligerent episodes of not allowing anyone to take my keys. I thought I was a much better driver when I was drunk.

Many drunks think this way until the worst finally happens. It isn't IF something bad happens when we drive drunk; it's WHEN it does. Many people in a progression of their drinking getting worse have a battle cry that includes not being as bad as someone they know who drinks more than they do. "I haven't been in jail. I haven't killed anyone. I haven't had a DUI or lost my job." Yet! Relying on those denials as a reason to keep drinking makes drinkers get worse, never better.

Although I didn't drink heavily every day, I woke up thinking about alcohol, planning on buying it and then drank in binges, which came closer and closer together. I had 28 years of binge drinking and it was progressing. Long gone were the days when drinking was fun, calming, or carefree. All bets were off as to what would happen. Most often, there was some form of drama where I was the one in trouble. Not every time I drank did I end up in trouble, but when I was in trouble, it was always a direct result of drinking. For those of us who struggle with any addiction or addictive behaviors, the trouble starts when we lose the choice to stop.

After five years of telling Dr. Hepler-Smith that I drank occasionally, I blurted out, "I drink... a lot". This was to stave off any further thought on her part to pronounce me insane... Bipolar. I had to control this whole thing somehow. I couldn't be mentally ill. What would my life look like now as a labeled reject of society? How could I "do" my life anymore? They (not sure who) would take my kids, and I would be shunned by my friends and relatives for all time. Alcohol had been my answer to "Am I going to be okay?" for many years. It may have helped in some way at certain times in my life when anxiety threatened to take over completely. But, isn't that why we do any addictive behaviors? Am I going to be okay? Yes, if I have enough of whatever has worked for me in the past...alcohol, drugs, money, food, bingeing, starving, affording us the opportunity to feel better, even if for a very short time. Who knows what addiction we are prone to that might just get us through some horrible times of prolonged stress and anxiety?

"So, what you're telling me," stated Dr. Hepler-Smith, "is that for these past five years while you have been my patient, you've been drinking like this."

"Yes," I proclaimed, as if in front of a jury finally telling the truth about a very big part of my life.

Honesty had never been very high on my priority list, although I acted a good part when I felt it was needed. I learned to do that early in my life. Growing up in alcoholism or with any addictive behaviors from parents lends itself to lying and manipulating the truth so as not to get into big trouble and, sometimes, in my case, not get beaten. Dr. Hepler-Smith knew of my intense fears of going crazy, although irrational until now. The scenarios I played out for her in most sessions left her wondering how to treat such high levels of anxiety. She had prescribed a variety of medications without knowing I was drinking heavily all along. Now, Dr. Hepler-Smith and I began the journey of finding what medication I could take that would not be habit forming.

In my early years of drinking, I had a fear of taking medications and refused to take pills. It was alcohol that became my very best friend. The issue now was that the antidepressants she had been prescribing were not working. They don't, if one drinks like I did. The nasty "what if" scenarios I created in my mind, day and night, about what was going on in my life were sending me over the edge. I didn't believe alcohol was the culprit when I made my announcement to her that day, but it was worth a try. I would do anything not to be pronounced insane. I didn't know quitting drinking was the answer and that my life would change immeasurably for the better. I never cared who knew I was an alcoholic; just don't tell anyone I am crazy. Now that I know getting sober is the answer, I'll yell it from the highest mountain tops to anyone and everyone.

I took Dr. Hepler-Smith's suggestions of attending 12 Step meetings seriously, going to inpatient rehab if I needed to detox and finding a sponsor. I reached out and got the help I needed. Dr. Hepler-Smith was gracious, firm, and kind. She gave me hope to get my life back by saying that once I began recovery in earnest, we would take a look at the Bipolar diagnosis again within the next year to 18 months.

That I was a danger to society was not the issue that got me to change my life. At that time, I couldn't care less. I felt as though I was taking on the bravado of my father and his generation. I became invincible once I began drinking. I drank because I liked the way it made me feel. That's it. I wasn't blaming anyone for anything. I did, however, want to be strong and powerful like my Dad. I had always loved him beyond measure as well as Mom. The fact that he and I, from my beginning, were in direct conflict for her attention was what got in the way.

As many people think, I thought doing things my way or on my own was my answer. Reaching out for help was only for people who were weak. The message I had gotten throughout the years was "don't get help; handle it on your own."

My reason for becoming a member of a 12 Step Recovery Program was because I didn't want to be the woman I was becoming. I began by going online to find 12 Step meetings in my area. I had no idea how much help and support is out there! I went to meetings, found a better way to "do" life, and over the course of the next few years, little by little, things got better. I learned, one day at a time, to grow up. I hated every minute of realizing I wasn't all powerful and was stunned to come to the realization I had considered myself to be my own god. I was told in the meetings that the good thing about being in a 12 Step program is that we grow up; the bad thing is that we do it in public. It was all about change, truly changing most of the "guidance" my head was giving me about me. How do I leave what's familiar, even though it's sick and bad for me, and trust others based on how they stay clean and sober one day at a time? I did it; I had to. The hardest part for anyone who needs help is to reach out for it and I am glad I did.

In 12 Step Recovery, my goal was and is about the possibility of growing into a better person and having the ability to live a sober life without any mind altering substances. Each and every time I attend a meeting, it is about support; that's it. It is less about preventing drinking for me and more about an existence free from resentment, jealousy, and guilt.

After my first year of sobriety, which was very early in recovery, I thought about going back to college. During the last year, I had gained a different perspective on anxiety and depression. Mental illness was not the monster around the corner I thought it was. I realized we ALL have it in some form or another. "Am I going to be okay?" is a question all humans have. There was nothing wrong with me! Holy shit!

I wanted to do graduate work in something I had dreamed of doing but couldn't imagine being sane enough to do...psychology. When watching the movie, *Sybil*, I was in the depths of despair in identifying with the character, Sybil. I wanted to be like her therapist, Dr. Wilbur, who stuck by her and helped her find a way out of her mental illness. My hope in that summer of 2005, as I began my graduate program, was to learn to be something like Dr. Wilbur.

I took one graduate course at Duquesne University during the summer to see if I could read and retain more than a magazine article. I found out I could. The course was "Human Growth and Development." I loved it!

In late November of 2007, I was 50 years old and my deepest, darkest fears were being realized. I was in my last year of Graduate school. I had separated from Chet the year before and he had moved to an apartment near Best Tile. Our son, Chetty, was in his senior year of high school, aimlessly planning to do nothing after graduation. Katherine was heading into a clinical depression and so was I.

The weekend after Thanksgiving of that year I asked Missy, a friend from Recovery, to drive me to the Psych Ward at Allegheny

General Hospital in Pittsburgh. By that time, Dr. Hepler-Smith and I had tried every kind of anti-depressant and anti-anxiety medication she could find that was non-narcotic. I was suicidal. I had found myself in the cycle of wanting to die but not wanting to kill myself, then wanting to kill myself but not wanting to die.

I was sitting in a little room in the ER with a nurse evaluating me. She asked if I was suicidal. My answer was "Yes." Then I added, "Your scissors look good right now."

Here I was, in the very place I had hoped to avoid my entire life. There was no way out but through this experience. Once upstairs on the locked down wing of the psych ward, I began receiving the intensive therapy I had needed so very long ago. I was given a new medication, attended daily group therapy sessions for a week, and many tests were performed. The doctors here discovered that my mental illness had been exacerbated by my entering into menopause the year before.

I had been distraught that I was three years sober and still found myself in line to get my daily dose of psych medications like everyone else on my floor. Wasn't I supposed to be all better by then?

By the end of the week, instead of locking me into a room where no one would ever see me again as I had feared, I left the psych ward at Allegheny General and began a different journey to wholeness. I had faced my deepest, darkest fear of going insane. Once I knew what was happening to me, I was able to come out of the darkness and into my own light.

In December of 2008, I graduated with my Masters in Counseling Psychology. I did my thesis on Grief and Loss and its Impact on Addiction and Anxiety. Loss often brings people to therapy. What I believed I needed to do as a therapist was far less about the books and the theories I had studied at Duquesne than what I had experienced in life. What I have seen, heard, and mostly, how I have been treated gives me insight and wisdom. I wanted to have a private practice, helping people, especially adolescents and early 20-somethings, work through their most difficult and confusing times.

CHAPTER EIGHTEEN

Resisting The Curriculum

IN GRADUATE SCHOOL, I WAS REQUIRED TO TAKE A CLASS ENTITLED Psychological Testing as one of the main requirements to move forward with my dissertation. I had one of the most brilliant professors on the campus of Duquesne University, Dr. Geoffrey Miller, who is highly regarded in his field of psychological testing. The first day of class there were graduate and doctoral students all between the ages of 25 and 30 years old. Then there was me, struggling to figure out this complicated calculator I had just bought in the student bookstore.

When I looked up, Dr. Miller had already put some equation on the dry erase board for us to ponder and work on. As the rest of the class clicked away on their calculators, some not even looking down at what they were doing, I leaned over to a young man sitting next to me and asked, "How do I turn this on?"

I was totally lost from the first minute of that class…almost as lost as I was in Statistics, another course I was required to take before I could obtain my degree. By the time the midterm exams were given, I had four tutors and worked harder on this course than I had ever worked in any class before. It wasn't about my not considering all those numbers and figures important, although at times I didn't. It was that my very right-sided brain couldn't understand how coming up with an answer like -.38 to a long involved equation could help me help anyone else who was crippled with horrific anxiety. The day of the midterm, Dr. Miller handed out the exam. I took one look at it and started crying. The only parts I knew were about Darwin and the history of psych testing. I folded up the exam, collected my things, and handed what I had written to Dr. Miller, who was sitting in the hall outside the classroom.

He took one look at me and said not to worry about this, we would talk during the break at the next class. During that break, I walked up to Dr. Miller, who had the driest sense of humor of any-one I had ever met. I thought he could be a standup comedian as a side job and told him so. Deadpan in his reactions to me always, he gave me a slight raise of the eyebrow, and that was it.

"Dr. Miller, it's like this," I said. "In working toward your doc-torate, if you were required to take a tap dancing class, what would you think?"

"I'd fall," was his reply.

"Yes," I said, "but you would have to take that class with others who have been tap dancing since they were very young and knew all of the steps already."

He looked at me with full attention, still no sign of a smile or frown.

I continued, "You would have to take each class trying to keep up with what came as second nature to everyone else. No matter what, you'd do whatever it took to keep up. You'd have to take extra classes, possibly get another dance instructor to help as you headed toward your midterm and final."

His eyes were totally clear and focused, but there was a hint of a twinkle in them as if he knew where I was going with this.

"For the mid-term you'd have to do a recital and for your final there would be a solo performance required."

"I get it," he said. "Have a seat."

The fact about all of those equations is -.38 will not help me be able to help anyone. There are many academic articles and journals with long windy explanations of what is wrong with the 'mentally ill' filled with statistics rounded off to the nearest equation. What?!?!? To have life experiences similar to those who seek help from us, and to have survived by doing the work needed to grow from those experiences is what brings about change. It is from our experiences of pain, which lead to our passion, and then on to our purpose that we help others. People who come to my office seeking help share their stories that ultimately derive from how anxiety, in whatever form, has impacted and continues to impact their lives and the lives of those around them.

Anxiety, for example. The Diagnosis and Statistical Manual (DSM-V) gives us a multitude of codes required for professionals to diagnosis and then submit for approval from insurance companies.

The plethora of psychiatric and psychological material available to keep those of the academia tied up in their egos and appropriately detached is outstanding. What I refer to is not the inaccuracies of these codes, but the idea that most jails, rehabs, and hospitals are filled with lost, desperate people who see no way out other than what their minds come up with.

What we are doing as a national and psychological community at large, is not working. Watching the news, we hear broadcasters state that most of the criminals today had 'mental illness' as if that is unusual. Most of us have to deal with some form of mental illness, addiction, and grief either in ourselves, or in our families. Denial is the greatest killer of all.

> From around the age of three, a child is unable to handle anything more stressful than deciding who to play with next. Little ones don't have the emotional wherewithal to cope with the anxiety that might come from what they see, what they hear, and how they are treated. These messages from parents or caregivers early in our lives, whether comforting or horrifying, are embedded as emotional imprints within us for life. This causes us to begin to think of ourselves as worthwhile or not.

Most people have some form of anxiety that fuels their crises. In my experience, anxiety and depression filled most of my days. There were occasional times of relief or so-called well-being.

In his book, *Emotional Intelligence*, the author, Daniel Goleman states that anxiety flushes the frontal cortex with adrenaline, and our thoughts become like scrambled eggs. Let's take an analogy I often use with clients. Remember in school when you were sitting blissfully in a daydream and no one was wiser? Then, the teacher asked you to go to the board and do a math problem. You couldn't remember or even write your phone number! Anxiety clears out any thinking other than flight or fight. Once we sit back down in our seats, we know what the answer is. But not up there at that damn board. It is similar to when anxiety takes hold of us in any situation. Thinking clearly seems to elude us and fear runs the show. "Am I going to be okay?" is asked in a multitude of ways on a daily basis:

Within the framework of mental illness such as;

"I just had a panic attack."

"I feel like I'm going crazy."

"My mind isn't working right."

Within the framework of addiction;

"What if I don't have enough?"

"What if my parents find out?"

"What if my boss finds out?"

Within the framework of grief;

"My dad died."

"My mom died."

"My best friend committed suicide."

"My cat died."

"My girlfriend dumped me."

"My husband wants a divorce."

If a person comes from a family that doesn't talk about any of these things, the answer to "Am I going to be okay?" is "Not if we keep all the thoughts and feelings stuffed down deep inside and keep telling everyone we are fine."

Now that I have my private practice, I love what I do! I am passionate about the whole idea that none of us with addictions or addictive behaviors is a "piece of shit," although that's one of the core beliefs we often have. I heard in 12-Step Recovery "what others think of me is none of my business." I add, "What I think of me means everything." It gave me permission to be me and true to what that means. I used to wonder why I sometimes had such heaviness in my heart after hearing my client's stories. Was it because I carried their stories with me even after they had left my office? Or, was it because I was getting even more in touch with what was going on inside myself? One of the breakthroughs I had was that due to my life experiences, I attach myself to people even though my manner may seem detached. It explains why I have had trouble with relationships.

I have now accepted that all aspects of me are okay, even the not so good parts. What I once thought was a totally selfish concept - to think of me and my needs - is now called "self-care." What happened to me as a child was not my fault. What I do about it as an adult, how I live my life in the future, is my responsibility. My journey through recovery brought me to a place where I am confident I can help others.

CHAPTER NINETEEN

Having the Talk

AS I NEARED THE NEW YORK THRUWAY EXIT CLOSEST TO DELANSON, I didn't get off. They didn't live there anymore. That house was now someone else's home. The memories flowed as well as the tears, knowing that the important moments of Mom's death loomed just ahead... filling part of this day. I neared Clifton Park, where my parents now lived so they could be close to Denise and Diana and their families. It was amazing how my seven-hour drive from Cranberry Township to Clifton Park flew by with so many memories.

As I arrived at The Bentley, a senior high rise for those 55 and older, I parked my 2004 RAV 4 where my father could see I had arrived. He threw down the exterior door opener for me to get into the back lobby. It was so strange to come to see them here.

I caught the opener and went inside to see how Mom looked, dreading how things would be in that small condo they now called home. It still seemed so odd, even after the year and a half they lived in this place, to take an elevator up to the second floor to see my parents. For some reason, that part was off-putting to me each time.

The condo door was open, and when I walked in, I saw Mom sitting up on her sofa with her oxygen tube settled in her nostrils, like it belonged there. She smiled and said, "Hi!" Her voice was raspy, probably from the constant flow of oxygen drying her throat.

I went over and kissed her, sitting down next to her, where I wanted to be for as long as I could. Just as quickly as I had that thought, I wanted to be gone doing something else, somewhere else. Anything, but this. Anywhere, but here. I settled in to ask her the usual things about her breathing, walking and eating.

Mom had gained weight from the fluid buildup associated with congestive heart failure. Her doctors had her on a myriad of medicines to counteract the unforgiving progress of her symptoms.

At this stage, as I was seeing her for the first time in a few months. She looked good and was calm. Later in that first week, when Mom and I had time alone, she told me, "The hospice people say I'm dying." It was as though she wanted me to tell her something to strike that fact off the record and make it not so. I had come to her rescue so many times before, why not one last attempt by me to defeat this bit of info? The fact that she was dying had been determined by every professional on her team of doctors, nurses, and hospice care workers, and confirmed by Denise. I simply said, "Yes, Mom, that's what's happening."

My remark slipped from the conversation into some place where all comments went that Mom didn't like or agree with. No one was going to tell her what was happening and what wasn't. As her days went from holding her own to slipping into a morphine-induced daze and bunny sightings, Mom held court from her sofa. Dad paced from room to room (there were only three), looking for some way to change the course of this impending inevitable end.

I soon determined I wanted to spend time with Mom and not go anywhere else. I had brought a couple of magazines I thought she might like. One was on Queen Elizabeth's Jubilee Year celebration and another about Grace Kelly and Jackie Onassis. She looked at them without acknowledging them and went back to playing *Solitaire* on the TV tray in front of her. The Food Channel played non-stop in the background.

Solitaire is something I do as well, only now I play on my laptop or iPhone. It helps soothe me and takes my mind off other things. It had always worked for Mom.

She also played the game, *Trouble*, with whoever would play with her. First, it was with us children when the twins and Dave were in high school. Later, she played against her grandkids until she developed a bump on her thumb from pushing the bubble that made the dice jump to a random number. *Trouble* was then tossed out and *Solitaire* became her game of choice.

She played with a 20-year-old, worn deck of cards that felt and looked more familiar to her than anything in that new condo they called home. There were pieces of furniture they had kept from the old house that fit nicely - first and foremost, as you might expect, the sofa. This one was dark blue with tiny little squares of country colors in a pattern on the fabric. It felt good to have these things here to carry all of us from the one place to the other. Photos, end tables, bedding and dishes all helped with the transition of having this be the place to come when we wanted to be with our parents. Mom seemed to be okay, and for now, I was, too.

Denise and Diana had tried for several years to get Mom and Dad to consider moving away from Delanson into a maintenance-free living situation. Neither would hear of it. Denial continued to reign supreme, but after the flood of 2010, we kids got together to stage an intervention of a kind. None of us were prepared to continue running to their rescue, especially when it meant endangering our lives. Denise said it was time to call in the "big guns" and confront Dad head on. By "big guns," she meant me.

Each of my sisters had played an amazing part in the care and upkeep of our old house and our parents in the five years or so before they moved. Dina was not altogether on board with the move because of the stress it would put on our parents and on us as well.

We all sat around that infamous dining room table with Mom and Dad to see what kind of mood they were in and how difficult this was going to be. Always tiptoeing around both of them, I had decided not to tiptoe anymore.

Mom's progressing symptoms of congestive heart failure (CHF) had put her in a passive place. Dina's son, Tyler, would say she was "loopy." She was loving and kind and would answer my questions simply by saying "Yes." We were told that the lack of oxygen in her blood made this change in her disposition. In some ways, we were lucky because some people become very difficult and mean at this point of CHF, but her sweeter disposition created confusion for us.

At the dining room table, Denise went over Mom and Dad's finances. Mom had handled the money from early in their marriage. When Dad had taken care of the finances, they lost their car and nearly lost their house. Once Denise finished, we asked Dad to come down to the basement.

In that damp, smelly basement, I faced Dad and told him we had decided it was time for them to move.

"Absolutely not," he reacted. "No one is going to tell me to leave this house. We have already told you kids we are staying and dying here."

His German temper began to escalate, and my old anxiety coping mechanism of wanting to escape to my room kicked in. I fought it and faced Dad. I made him listen to me. "You had Dina and Adam drive out here to help in one of the most dangerous floods this area has seen! My sister almost got killed coming out to help you!"

Denise and Diana were silent and somewhat shocked. None of us had ever spoken to Dad that way, and I was ready to have the "Nazi guard" in him come out and attempt to demolish me. He looked at me as though I was his worst enemy. I stood my ground. It was a momentous time for me and I finally, at the age of 55, was able to tell my father "NO" and "I DON'T AGREE!"

He started to cry and I attempted to hug him. He was as stiff as a plank of wood. I stepped back and Diana said, "Let her hug you, Dad."

I realized that day that these two people, my parents, had not grown a bit emotionally since they were in high school, maybe even grade school. And really, how would they? Fear had kept them safe in their very small world, and now, we were threatening to force them into the big, bad world.

I went upstairs where Mom and Dina were sitting at the table making small talk. The twins and Dad came up a bit later, and Dad said, "I think it's time we sold the house."

Really! Do you now?

Off and on, I had been in conflict with my father my entire life, especially now. I loved this man more than any other man in my life, and yet, there was turmoil in my soul whenever I was around him. Such a big part of me could not stand him, and it always got in my way. From early on, he called me stubborn if I didn't follow how he wanted things to go. I didn't care about him like I cared about Mom. He just bothered me, probably because he had scared me so much in my early years with his outbursts of anger.

Although Dad was always happy to see whoever had come to see them, he tried his best to be okay with what was happening around him but constantly struggled with how to handle what might happen next. I saw how strong denial could be as these next four weeks unfolded.

I went to leave my stuff at Diana's house that was about 15 minutes away from the condo. Immediately, I found a 12-Step Recovery meeting list online. We can find meetings all over the world, even in Clifton Park, New York. It was what I needed...to be with people who had gone through what I was going through and not relapse. Amazing how that works.

From the beginning of man, there has been some way to escape reality. The spectrum of addiction goes from having one or two of something to relax to never having enough to be okay. Without the support of the meetings and fellowship of the people in the 12 Step program in Clifton Park, this would have turned out to be a far different narrative. This is no joke. The answer to all of our "Am I Going to Be Okay?" desperate pleas from the bottom of our guts doesn't have a chance in hell if left to our own devices. No longer do I answer that question by any means other than reaching out to someone who understands what I'm going through. 12 Step Recovery is a program which began in the early 1930s in Akron, Ohio and has stood the test of time. The 12 Step method helped me accept the unacceptable of life.

I had never been at the end of my mother's life before. I needed to know I could call people I had just met in a meeting and have their experience, strength, and hope guide me emotionally and physically.

Recovery isn't about not drinking, using, eating, spending, sexing, sexting, gambling and so on. It is about how to get through these real-life times when what used to work is no longer an option.

Nothing and no one else can possibly be the answer, especially family. It just isn't possible.

My family members were going through their own emotional ups and downs. They couldn't help me with my emotional pain. They were dealing with their own pain. This is the hell of staying isolated within a family system where we were taught not to talk about the emotions we experience.

My siblings and I have always been extremely close; yet, I couldn't go to any of them to share how it felt to want to dive into a swimming pool of bourbon manhattans with a truckload of cherries dumped in. They wouldn't get it. They haven't been there. The idea of one person in recovery helping another because he or she has been in that place or situation is what the premise of Recovery is all about. It's not a cult or a religion. There's nothing to fear. I needed to know how to deal with my emotions and stay sober. My years spent in 12 Step Recovery had given me the miracle of living through many difficult times. I had been trying to find the desired answer to the question "Am I going to be okay?" with sobriety and growth instead of relapsing into the "I don't give a shit" despair.

After leaving Diana's, I went to the 5 p.m. meeting just down Route 146 from the condo. I met people with whom I am still in contact today. That is how it works. We open ourselves up to strangers who often become connections we trust. I hung out with amazing women with all different types of personalities, some more helpful than others, but all there for me just the same. Also, there was an older fellow, Bob, who played an integral part in my "okayness" throughout my time in Clifton Park.

This support network is what is responsible for my remaining sober through these weeks before and after Mom's death. Clifton Park afforded me a variety of meetings to find the people to support me every day at whatever time I needed it. I didn't know any of them when I arrived, but I could relate to each one of them with the human condition we all brought to each meeting. Each one of us hoped to do things differently than we had done before and like no one we had ever known before. This is the reason I was able to remain open, sober, and accepting of each episode as it unfolded in the remaining days of Mom's life.

"Why do I need to get help when there's nothing wrong?" is the call of everyone steeped in deep denial about what is going on right under their very noses. Within ourselves and our families, things have to get so bad that the bottom we reach is most often beyond despair. Adolescent suicide, drug overdoses and escapism of all kinds is running the show in this country, as it is in many areas around the world. How can I do the work that I do without doing my own? I am no hypocrite.

I didn't hit the lowest of bottoms myself before I decided to change most everything in my life. I didn't have a DUI, didn't lose a business, family or friends and wasn't even empowered with the pride of being the worst as I began to attend meetings. But, all of those things that hadn't happened to me, just hadn't happened "yet".

We all think we can decide how far down the ladder, scale or what have you, we are willing to go. But, there comes that time when we lose that choice. Then, we are in denial for the sake of denial.

So, the cry of all of us who are in denial demands that what is happening is not happening! Sometimes this goes on until there is no voice left, and we see clearly the life of denial leads us all to be the only ones not seeing what everyone else clearly sees.

It would be great if doing recovery on our own worked as well. Many people come into a recovery program and leave within a few weeks, months or even a couple of years believing they are now cured, have all they need to go out and do life on their own, their way. My way got me a seat in the rooms and given enough time, my way would have gotten me killed. If persons on their own could accomplish recovery, the treatment centers, hospitals, jails, and cemeteries wouldn't be full.

I was overwhelmed with sadness and anxiety throughout my life, a roller coaster of emotions that led me to think I was going insane. The message of nothing being acceptable, other than happy smiling, was clear throughout my life. The oft-spoken, "What's wrong now?" asked by my parents, and then eventually, school teachers, Sunday school teachers, and once, a priest during mass. (How embarrassing!) Then, it came from friends, who eventually pushed me away thinking there was something wrong with me. The message I heard was clear. I was NOT okay and had very little hope of ever getting an affirmative answer to the question my mother and I so often asked "Am I going to be okay?"

CHAPTER TWENTY

Dealing With The Hard Stuff

DURING THAT FIRST WEEK IN CLIFTON PARK, A VISITING NURSE FROM the hospice staff came to take Mom's vitals and check on her. This was my first encounter with someone from hospice and I had lots of questions. She suggested I call Saratoga Hospice and have someone who would be on Mom's team inform us as to what to expect. I did make that call. The nurse who would lead the team made an appointment to meet us at the condo. When she arrived, Dina and Dave were on speakerphone while Denise, Diana, Katherine and I sat in the living room. Our hope was to have an orientation on how the process of hospice and this whole death thing worked. It was not as I thought it would be. We had been told by Mom's doctors she MIGHT last a month. However, the nurse stated Mom could last from six months to two years. She was confused as to why she was even there meeting with us.

WHAT?!?! I was incredulous. When I get on my high horse, it's ugly. I got into a kind of debating match with the head nurse of

Mom's case, who was vague and not helpful. Thankfully, this person didn't end up being head nurse throughout Mom's last weeks.

As I had previously experienced the death of my friend, Luisa, I felt once again the panic of losing a loved one. The hospice nurse was saying most of the care will be given by the family. Mom and Dad were in the other room, not interested in any part of this. Dad was counting out pills, making sure that Mom would get her water pills so she wouldn't gain any weight.

He had done an amazing job of taking care of Mom in that way through these last few years. Of course, none of us ever really knew what he was doing up there in Delanson since they told us very little about what was actually going on.

It had been the call from Dr. Burton to me that gave us the information we needed to take over the care of Mom and Dad. It had to be subtle because Dad was all about power and control. It was not only the traits of alcoholism that brought this out in him; his personality was that way. His early childhood years were filled with much heartache, pain and suffering as most children of the Depression experienced. Dad was a handsome, blonde, blue-eyed, perfect German youth. He had the ability to be cold and calculating as well as flip to funny and somewhat loving. He was more generous than Mom, but he had an addictive quality to his spending. That's why Mom had taken over the finances years earlier. Joint checking accounts didn't work for them.

After talking with Dr. Burton for more than an hour, I called Denise, Diana and Dina about the truth of it all. I also called Dave, who lived in Discovery Bay, California, with his wife and daughter. We were all blown away that things weren't fine with Mom, as Dad had said. His comments to us about her failing health, episodes of fainting, and frequent trips to the bathroom (which she sometimes didn't make in time), were always followed with, "Oh, those doctors don't know what they're talking about. They want her to go through all of these tests, and she doesn't want them. Why put her through having a chest X-ray when it makes her claustrophobic?"

I sat there listening to the hospice head nurse telling us what we could expect to go through as Mom became sicker. I replied, "All of her doctors are telling us she has less than six months to live. She will need more care than what you are telling us that hospice can give! None of us have medical backgrounds! We will need more than an occasional person randomly here for an hour each day!"

I became irate, as fear and sadness surged to the surface. I had seen what Luisa required in her end of life care, and this was not something we were qualified to take on. The hospice nurse stated that, in time, it would, indeed, get more difficult but not to worry, we could do it. After all, it was Mom's wish to stay at home. The nurse was emphatic. Since there was a very long waiting list for the few hospice care centers in the area, all signs pointed to we were "it."

Later that afternoon, after the hospice worker left, Denise and I spoke about what she had said. It was hard for me to express my concern over what was coming without creating any friction between Denise and me. Diana was vocal as well, but Denise tended to take charge, thankfully, and had been the one to make the decisions for Mom and Dad for a very long time. There was nothing else we could do.

In those last few days of Mom's life, the reality set in as to how difficult her care was and the toll it was taking on us. But, by then, we were in it too deeply, and it had to play itself out.

One of the worst parts of Congestive Heart Failure is the loss of kidney functioning and the fluid buildup in the patient's body. Mom gained weight by the day and every effort had been taken to increase the diuretics to stave off this part. Mom's one responsibility each day was to weigh herself. She wouldn't do it. That was reality and she would have no part of it. No one could tell her what to do, except maybe Dad if he yelled at her loud enough.

The hospice workers had been encouraged to get to know Mom a little bit better so they could see what we were talking about with her not being compliant and truthful. My daughter, Katherine, was visiting Mom when one of the nurses came in to check on her.

"Judy?" asked the nurse of my Mom, "Have you been weighing yourself?"

"Oh, yes," said Mom, lying through her teeth.

Katherine, ever the truth sayer and advocate of right and wrong, shouted, "Grandma, you have not!"

Mom sat back sheepishly, as she would do when caught in her lies.

"Is this true?" asked the nurse.

"Well, I thought I did."

Mom became like a three-year-old, whenever convenient, stating the scale they were using didn't work. Dad came to the rescue and started to explain why the scale was wrong. "Those damn ceramic tiles in that goddamn bathroom are installed wrong, and her weight is not right on that scale. I had to go out and buy two new scales just to get her right weight!" Dad had bought new scales. Then he shoved them from tile to tile in Mom's bathroom to find a weight that was either the same as the day before or less.

The hospice team looked at us and seemed to get it, finally. They were dealing with something different than they thought…three-year-olds in 78 year-old bodies.

Later in the day, after the hospice team left, I sat with Mom and spoke with her about her decision to remain home and not go to the hospital as things progressed. We were all careful not to say anything about the possibility of death, as she and Dad didn't want to hear or believe those words.

"Mom," I said, "I want you to know that the twins, Dina and I are willing to take care of you at home through this whole thing, but you have to know how difficult this will be on all of us."

I thought it was time for some reality checking with her. If anything, she and I had progressed in our relationship to being honest with each other. I wasn't interested in saving her from the truth or reality anymore. It was time for her to take part in some of this, even if it was only having the understanding as best she could, the toll it would take on all of us, especially emotionally. "I love you and will do whatever it takes to help you through this, but you have to know, Mom, how hard this will be for all of us." I wasn't tearful at all or mean or cruel either. It was time for open, honest sharing with a person who was uncomfortable with that.

I was looking directly at Mom's face and she had no real reaction or response other than to say, "Yeah." That was that.

The next day, Mom and Dad had planned for a priest from the neighboring St. Stephen's Catholic Church to come say prayers and talk with them. I wanted to be a part of it.

I had reconnected with an old high school boyfriend, Will. He was a great support and distraction as well. We shared stories of days gone by and a love of the Adirondacks, particularly Long Lake, New York. I had been staying with him for a few nights and had left his house on my way to the condo to pray. I called Denise who was already there. We had made a schedule of who would be there during the mornings to afternoon and who would be there in the evenings to put them to bed. That eventually progressed to someone remaining overnight.

Dad didn't want anyone taking over what he felt was his job… giving Mom her meds and helping her to the bathroom. Then I called Denise to let her know I was on my way, she said, "Something's going on with Dad."

"What?" I asked.

"Well, he and I were talking, and his face went white. He is sweating a lot." She went on to describe that he was unable to remember why hospice papers were there on the small wooden kitchen table, which was now station central for medicines and medical information. Denise said Dad was acting weird, and she didn't know what was wrong. I sat upright in the car and said, "Call an ambulance, I'll be right there. I'm only about 10 minutes away."

Denise said, "Oh, we don't need an ambulance. He'll be fine."

Because of learning through recovery not to jump into my high levels of reaction any longer, I was able to keep my mouth shut and repeat I'd be right there. I was so frustrated with her response.

Let me address the reality of what Denise had already gone through with Mom and Dad for the past two years. Dina, Denise and Diana had been the ones who either drove out the far distance to Delanson every time there was a crisis or emergency or met them at Ellis Hospital when either Mom or Dad had an episode of anxiety or whatever it turned out to be. So, Denise's reaction to this particular incident with Dad was based on past history in dealing with him. She had been coping with a tremendous amount of stress taking care of them. I, the hero Viking coming to save the day, was so mad!

{ 🐦 }

CHAPTER TWENTY-ONE

Have They All Gone Crazy?

I PULLED INTO THE FRONT PARKING LOT WHERE I COULD COME IN through the main doors without Dad tossing me the keys. Dale, the wonderful guy who managed the high rise, was always somewhere near the front door as his office was to the right of it. He let me in and I said, "I think something might be wrong with my dad." He and Dad were buddies, so Dale said, "Let me know what I can do."

I went to the elevator and felt another layer of anxiety of "Am I going to be okay" settle in. As I approached their condo, the door was wide open, and Mom was sitting on the sofa with panic on her face.

"Oh, Debbie, something's wrong with Daddy," she said.

"Where is he?" I asked, "and why is the door wide open?"

Mom explained in her panicked voice that Dad had some kind of episode where he couldn't remember anything, and he looked terrible. She was afraid for him.

"Where is Dad?!" I asked, trying to make sense of this scene of her alone on the sofa in a complete panic with the ever-present oxygen hose hanging out of her nose.

"He went to meet Della Mae." Della Mae was one of their class-mates from high school who had graduated with them. When she comes from Florida to visit her family, she always stops in and says hi to Mom and Dad.

"What?" I shouted. I was asking that a lot.

Mom said Della Mae had heard how sick Mom was and wanted to come over and see them. Dad had told her he would drive to meet her at the Panera Bread down the road.

Somehow, being clueless as to where he was or what was happen-ing, he found the place and Della Mae. Then, due to his confusion, took longer than usual to get back home. Mom was panicking and I sat down by her. I asked the obvious question, "Where's Denise?"

Mom said, "She went to get a pedicure at Happy Feet."

"Happy Feet!" I shouted. "What?"

Supposedly, after Denise had gotten off the phone with me, she said she was going to keep her appointment for a pedicure at Happy Feet and would be right back. That was before Della Mae's phone call and Dad's disappearance. I was trying to take this all in as I sat near Mom, swimming through the escalation of both of our emo-tions, when we heard Dad's booming voice coming from down the hall. He and Della Mae had just gotten off the elevator.

What a relief it was to see them both coming into the condo, safe and sound. At least that crisis was solved. Dad came to me and looked like he was near death. He was panicked and wanted to know if he was going to be okay. He kept saying over and over, "I don't under-stand what's going on."

Della Mae looked as if she thought she had made a big mistake in visiting but said, "Hi," and sat down to talk with Mom who was beginning to calm down.

Dad and I talked for a few minutes before I made the decision to get an ambulance. I called down to Dale and asked him to call one for Dad. He told me, "Sure will, but I just was going to call up there. I have a priest down here who says he's here to meet with your family."

I had forgotten all about the priest and the praying thing. "I'll bring Dad down," I said to Dale, "and bring the priest up."

When I told Dad that I had gotten him an ambulance, he said, "Good." Any other time in his life, he would've refused it. I think that's what Denise must have always experienced with Dad -- his refusal to cooperate – and she figured there was no way he would get in an ambulance. But now, as he felt things getting worse, he stood up and we left.

I told Mom that I was taking Dad downstairs to get in the ambu-lance, and I would also bring the priest up to see her. Mom seemed preoccupied with Della Mae and said, "Ok. I love you, hon."

What?!! Now, I knew her oxygen levels must be dangerously low!

She called out something to Dad, which she did from time to time, but he didn't hear her. His hearing was poor and he was in a state of confusion. We walked slowly down the hall into the elevator. All the while, I watched to see if he was on the verge of collapse.

"I can't figure out what's going on," Dad said. "I don't understand what's happening." He repeated this over and over as we got to the main floor and down the hallway to Dale's office. Dad recognized people. That wasn't the issue. I was thinking maybe this was a stroke of some kind. Dad sat down on the bench in the lobby as Dale and the priest came over to him.

"Hey, Dick, what's going on?" asked Dale as he looked up at me and said, "Definitely need an ambulance."

I introduced myself to Father Ben as he was also attempting to be of some aid to Dad. At that moment, the ambulance drove up to the front door of the complex and two paramedics came into the lobby to assess Dad's situation. They went back out to get the stretcher for Dad, saying he needed to get to the ER right away as his blood pressure was dangerously high. As was his way, Dad was trying to make a joke to soften the crisis. He often did that with people he'd just met.

Once they got Dad on the stretcher and were taking him out of the front door, Denise came running through the lobby from the elevator. She had returned from Happy Feet and wanted to go with Dad in the ambulance. I wanted to be the one to see this scene through to the end and let Denise go sit upstairs with Mom and the priest. I asked the ambulance driver if he was going to leave right this second. He said they would be leaving in a few minutes, so I took this opportunity to take the priest up to Mom and come right back down.

By the time we walked into that still open door of the condo, Della Mae had gone (quick visit), and Mom was sitting there waiting for either news of Dad or the priest. Mom was her B-movie drama self as the priest went over to her and sat by her side. She loved the attention.

I told her that Denise would be right back as the ambulance was here, and I wanted to go with Dad. They didn't take notice, either of them, as I slipped out, closed the door and went down to the lobby. Dad and Denise were in the ambulance and I was left to go back upstairs and pray.

I could feel myself having an inner struggle with wanting things my way, but this wasn't the time for any of that. It was fine that Denise went with Dad. I thanked Dale for all of his help and talked with him a bit longer than I needed to, but finally went upstairs.

When I went into the condo, only Mom was there. Father Ben had left. I asked, "Did you guys finish already?" Mom stated, "Yes, and you know what…he kissed me right on the mouth. I think he wanted me."

"No," I stated, waiting for this to sink in. Was she kidding? No, she wasn't, and would tell this tale to anyone who would listen until she literally couldn't talk any longer.

"No, Mother, he did not want you," I said. "He kissed you out of kindness. That's what priests do."

"Not this one," she stated. "He kissed me on the mouth, and I think he loves me."

"Yes, Mom, you already said that. In case you're interested, Dad left in the ambulance and Denise went with him. She's going to call us when they find out what's going on with him."

"Oh, good," Mom said, still in her reverie of finally finding true love with the priest who had come to pray for her errant soul. She went into complete detail of how kind he was and how loving he had been to her. "He kissed me right on the mouth," she repeated. I started to giggle at that point, and she smiled at me, loving all of it.

I said to her, "Mother, you slut."

She calmly stated, "I know. Isn't it awful?"

Preparing for Mom's death held its own denial in my mind as well. As the days progressed, and her mobility declined, we all took turns caring for her, along with hospice guiding us how to do what none of us wanted to do. Each sign of the nearness of Mom's death was acknowledged but tucked away somewhere in my mind. "Maybe she will stay this way for longer," I thought.

The clear memories of those few weeks before Mom died, the twins, Dina, and I share openly now whenever we get together. Most of the talks are hilarious with each one of us telling our part of some high drama of Mom beginning to reluctantly take her leave.

About two weeks before Mom died, the hospice workers told her they were going to be bringing in a hospital bed soon. They felt she would be more comfortable than she was leaning on her right arm, lying on her right side on the left corner of the sofa. She said, "No."

The longer the hospice workers stuck around, the more they began to see what we were talking about with handling Mom. She was not going to get off the sofa for anyone. She could not have cared less that her elbow slipped off the arm of the sofa every minute or so as she slept. Her body was showing signs of sores in many areas making it impossible for her to rest comfortably in a place where she had been safe her entire life.

One seemingly simple remedy was for us to shift Mom to her left side on the right side of the sofa. Umm, nope. As we attempted to shift her body to sit upright and then lay down on her left side, she flailed her arms and panicked, as if someone was taking her to face a firing squad. Actually, she would have preferred and been calmer with that scenario than leaving her spot.

On the day of Dad's episode, Mom and I waited to see how things went at the ER. Both the twins and Dina had gathered at the ER to see the results of all the tests. I was sure it was something stroke-like, but the ER doctors said it was Transient Global Amnesia which is a sudden, temporary episode of memory loss. During an episode of this type of amnesia, your recall of recent events simply vanishes, so you can't remember where you are or how you got there. In addition, you may not remember anything about what's happening in the here and now. Consequently, you may keep repeating the same questions because you don't remember the answers you've just been given. You may also draw a blank when asked to remember things that happened a day, a month or even a year ago. That explained Dad's odd behavior.

Dad remained confused and couldn't remember much of anything throughout the remaining time before Mom passed away and for some time after. He did, however, ask us over and over again about what happened as if to help him bring back any memory of that day and make sense of it all. We were on a whole new level now. Both parents were incapable of taking care of themselves, each in a different way. As I look back, I can see this was his way of protecting himself from the pain of watching Mom decline.

Even though they had fought terribly since their first meeting, their love was everlasting. There was love, dependence, fear and history that kept them together, and it worked. They were in their 56th year of marriage and totally absorbed in their drama and each other. It was difficult to get them to see there was anyone else in the house, except as their audience.

CHAPTER TWENTY-TWO

The Tough Job of Making Changes

CHANGING A BEHAVIOR TAKES A LOT OF WORK AND DEDICATION.
When I wanted to stop smoking back in my early twenties, I did so
"cold turkey." I had motivation since Chet and I were dating and he
was adamantly against smoking. I hung out with people who didn't
smoke, and even when I was drinking, which is when I had previously
smoked the most, I stayed mostly with people who didn't smoke,
including Chet.

*Often people think they can stop doing something harmful by just
stopping, not realizing they had been doing it to alter their moods. We
have done so many other things on our own, why not stop drinking,
smoking, drugging, eating the way we do, spending, and so on, by ourselves? It's like learning a new language or moving to a country where
one has no idea how to do the simplest things. Giving up a behavior
or habit that has been the answer to 'Am I going to be okay,' is no easy
task. The drink, gamble, high, shopping spree person responds by sending the message "Yes, you are going to be okay. There are enough cigarettes, alcohol, chocolate, and so on."*

To give up an addiction, help is needed, especially support from others who are going through or have gone through the same things. We need a guide, a way to see how it is done. One of the most important messages for anyone in addiction is that we can NOT recover on our own. Every one of us tries to do it our way. Like learning to speak another language, recovery from addiction might be academically learned by reading a book about it. Even listening to Rosetta Stone would be helpful for another language, yet, to converse fluently, one must practice on a daily basis with others who already know that language. We must have guides on how to handle the emotional impact of not drinking drugging, binging, or purging, gambling, sexing, or spending all we have.

Change means dedication to not going back to what's familiar. It means not only knowing, intellectually, there will be no more drinking, smoking, or binge eating, but also taking on the much more difficult emotional and physical challenges of avoiding those behaviors. Even if we know how much we will lose if drinking and driving happens again, or if we resume smoking when we have cancer or if we eat sugar filled foods when we have diabetes, the emotional yearning for and physical cravings of the habit will overpower any thought of the consequences. Addiction is far more powerful than any willpower can imagine.

The only way to change for any of us is to practice with others how to incorporate that change, one day at a time. When attempting to practice another way of living, another way of being that is overwhelmingly unfamiliar, waves of fear wash over us. Questions of "what if" overtake the journey to change and it seems easier, less fearful to revert to the old behavior. Medical bills rise; death looms. The insanity becomes evident in how much "safer" we think it will be to drink that fear and anxiety away. We can eat or starve ourselves to the point where "now everything will be okay."

"I don't want to" were words Mom often said during those last weeks of her life. She said this about weighing herself, walking when she was still able, and eating healthy. Her cravings were for cheeseburgers and French fries until she couldn't swallow any longer. Dad would dutifully give her a banana and some oatmeal in the morning to give a nutritional start to the day, and she didn't mind that. Any food after that was to be what she wanted, even though it was bad for her.

When the hospice staff finally realized Mom was refusing to do what was necessary to live longer and feel better, they told us they could do nothing other than come in briefly in the mornings to help get her to the bathroom. She refused to use the adult potty chair sitting next to the hospital bed she despised. The nurses told us she wouldn't last much longer because she was not participating in getting better.

They had no idea who they were dealing with. Mom was not about to have anyone tell her what to do at this stage of the game. That had never happened before, at least not without a fight, and it was not going to change. In her mind, she could keep doing what she had always done and everything would eventually be okay. Dad went along with her, sometimes reluctantly, most times barking at her in his frustration and fear of what lay ahead.

Mom ate the way she had always eaten. Throughout her life, she ate whatever she wanted unless she was attempting to lose weight. When she was on a diet, she would start out by following all the guidelines for healthy eating and exercise until she would succumb to a hot fudge sundae or a piece of pie. For years, Mom called out her requests from the safe confines of her right side on the left side of the sofa for whatever she craved to Dad's pissy-assed moods. Dad would bitch and swear, making it known to whoever could hear that he was the victim of her relentless demands. Yet, off he'd go to fulfill her wishes.

When Dad returned from the store or the kitchen with ice cream or pie, Mom would rise up just a slight bit and say, "Thank you, hon" and lie back into her world of herself. "Jesus Christ, Judy," Dad would bellow from his chair. He often yelled loudly at Mom for no reason. It's what he did. To attempt to change any of those behaviors at this late stage was useless. Throughout the years, neither of them saw a need for help from anyone outside of our family, and they saw no need for it now.

"How We Do Anything is How We Do Everything," a workbook written by Cheri Huber, speaks of doing the same things over and over again expecting different results. When we do the same thing in the same way, we will always get the same results whether that is anxiety, depression, loneliness and emotional pain and most times, we welcome it because it is familiar. It is too scary to do things differently. What would happen? We might die! We'd rather die, for sure, by doing what we are doing rather than to change.

In the case of anxiety and depression, the old stigma that remains to this day in many families is to keep secret that someone in our family needs mental health help. Every one of us in my family desperately needed help, but Dad refused to allow any of us to see therapists or doctors about these issues. The fear was, and remains to be, that something worse would happen if we got help. So, all of it was ignored, and we deteriorated into whatever state of anxiety and depression progressed. Silence was the answer. Always keep to yourself what your heartache and struggles are. The answer was to work harder and give into Mom's demands. We believed that was the key to her getting better and being okay.

Change means taking a look at what isn't working in our lives and making a decision to do something different in order to have a healthier, more peaceful way of life. Often, we are unable to see what we need to do to change, nor do we understand that we will have the support of others who have already made those changes. Nor, do we understand that there are gradual steps to a better way of living and when taken will make it all worthwhile. That's why most of us go back to what is familiar. It relieves the anxiety for a short time, but then things get worse...and the anxiety comes back.

CHAPTER TWENTY-THREE

Longing For Words I Never Heard

ON A HOT JULY AFTERNOON, I LEFT WILL'S HOUSE TO SPEND WHAT ended up being the last time with Mom when she was coherent and able to respond back. She had lost interest in everything she had once held important. She was at a very delicate balance of relief from pain through increasing amounts of morphine and Ativan to calm the surges of "Am I Going To Be Okay?" Anxiety now fully took over any moment it could without the defense of the fantasy world into which she had always retreated. Denial had no chance, as conditions worsened with Mom. It seemed Dad stayed confused, fortified with Scotch, pacing from one room to another trying as hard as he could, to avoid the truth of what was happening to Mom to sink in.

Mom's discomfort became very apparent in two-hour increments. We all took turns giving Mom the morphine that she hated. She knew what it meant. We did it. We had to and we wrote it down each time so that we would know when she needed more.

On a previous day, as I drove from Will's to their condo, I realized I was going emotionally numb. I was surprised that I wasn't crying all of the time like I thought I would. A state of denial of my own seemed to be setting in. We were now in a routine of doing things that seemed as if we had always done them. When hospice care began, there were parts of taking care of Mom that I was dreading: yet, now they felt normal. The landscape of upstate New York took on a new feel. Now, there was a familiarity, a sense of unison with all that surrounded me which became poignant as Mom's passing came closer.

There were sensory memories being made. I knew the smell and the feel of the weather would return to me with each year that passed and when her death anniversary would draw near. I was sensing that someday all of it would bring me back to these very last days of Mom's life. It seemed as though it couldn't be possible that the whole world wasn't on the same death bed vigil as we were.

I went up the elevator, which allowed me a short, two-floor ride of preparation to face whatever had transpired since I was there last. That elevator held promise of reprieve since I could be alone. Enclosed in a very private place, I could close my eyes, breathe, and give myself the stillness I needed in order to face whatever was happening in the condo.

The smells of medicine and strange odors hit me each time I exited that elevator, even before I opened their door. Mom was sitting up on the sofa. She had no idea that within a few days she would be taking the horrendous journey from this familiar place of safety to the horrors of becoming inseparable from that death trap of a hospital bed.

Denise was there and about to leave to do things she needed to do at home. Denise was always chipper and smiling, trying to make things seem as normal as possible. I sat down next to Mom. She was also smiling and enjoying the view from where she sat. I sat close, curled up into her body, as close as I could get and asked her how she was and what had happened that I had missed.

While we chatted about nothing really, I selfishly yearned for her to say loving words I had never heard from her. Mom and Dad said over and over how much they appreciated what we were all doing for them. Dad often said, "I don't know what we would do without you kids." And Mom would add, "Yes, that's right, Richard, we are lucky." (Dad was either Dicky or Richard to Mom, depending on her mood.)

During this time spent with her, I began to inwardly beg her, without outwardly asking, to ask me how I was doing. I kept thinking she would come to see how much everyone was doing for her, especially me. Near the end of her life, I hoped she would ask me, "Debbie, how are you doing with all you are going through and taking care of me?" I realized every one of us siblings had a major part in caring for Mom, but I needed her to recognize *me*. It was a lifetime of my yearning for her. I needed her to see me now. I would do whatever she needed, but she had to see me. I looked into her dying eyes over and over, silently begging her to ask me something about me.

It remained a fantasy wish, as I heard nothing unless I said it first. If I said, "I love you," she would say, "I love you, too." That was as much as I could expect. On this day, curled up next to Mom as

I used to do before all of the other kids were born, I took in whatever I could of her. Mom was quiet and seemed peaceful, allowing me near her. What I finally realized was that Mom was the love of my life, but I wasn't hers.

She was taking sips of water but no longer eating. Dad tried to give her a piece of banana. I sat across from her, watching her trying to chew it. She pretended to swallow. Dad said, "See, she swallowed it, right?"

"Mom, did you swallow it?" I asked. Mom nodded her head, but I could see she hadn't.

I said, "No, she didn't" and asked Mom if she still had it in her mouth. She nodded yes. It took a great deal of work on her part, but she finally swallowed it which ended up being the last piece of food she ate. It was scary to watch as I couldn't imagine how we would deal with her if she choked.

She was sipping water through a straw I held for her. She would answer, "I love you, too" back to my constant assertions of love. I'm sure she was at the point of being annoyed with me.

The old familiar yearning for my mother's love which I had pushed down deep inside through years of anger and disgust, came flooding back in these last few days. I couldn't get enough of her. No one else cuddled with her or loved her like I did. The twins and Dina kept their distance physically and emotionally. But, I would go to any length to have her notice me and know I was there. I had always wanted more of her than she could give me, especially now. She was never able to go past her self-focused survival mode that began when she was a three-year-old girl being walked away from her home and siblings, holding her mother's hand to be given away.

Two days before Mom died, the hospice nurse said she was in a coma. It was a Friday, and we were now shoving morphine in her mouth between her clenched teeth and wiping copious amounts of fluid from her mouth and nose. It was difficult and finally, the nurse gave us a patch so the fluids would dry up for a while.

It was all surreal at this point. Like we were caring for her but she wasn't Mom any longer. No communication, just taking care of what we thought she needed by way of pain relief and keeping her comfortable. Dina came when she could, but it seemed she was not into the end part of this. It was, indeed, overwhelmingly emotional to see Mom in this state. David called from California daily and cried each time he talked to any of us. Now that Mom was in a coma, he decided to fly to Albany.

On that Friday night, a few minutes before midnight, Dave's plane came in and Dad went to pick him up. When he walked through the front door into the condo, he went right to Mom and sobbed saying he wished he had come sooner. Even though he had talked to her each day, sometimes twice a day, he couldn't get over the fact that for the first time, he wouldn't hear her say something to him.

Their relationship had come a long way since the times when he was a child that I heard Mom saying hurtful, hateful things to him. Mom hated men, and she was not very fond of Dave. He and I seemed to get the brunt of her hatred when we were growing up. I am seven years older than Dave, so I went through it first, but I witnessed things he went through that no one should see or hear. Sometimes it is more harmful to witness abuse than to be abused.

Now, Mom and Dave had bonded, forgiven for whatever had happened, mostly by Dave toward her. Dave loved Mom with a passion, and once he got to her bedside and saw the state she was in, he never left her side. He slept on the sofa next to her bed the rest of that night. The rest of us went home to plan what to do the next day because it seemed that Mom was very close to death. The hospice staff said that she had 24 hours or less to live. What does someone do with that information? Now, what?

Denise and Diana began to get information from the funeral home in Delanson that Mom had selected. She was to be buried in Grove Cemetery, up the hill from the village of Delanson toward Quaker Street in a very small, beautiful wooded area. I had not been there since I was in the marching band in high school.

Each Memorial Day, we marched in the Delanson Memorial Day Parade from the high school down through the village of Delanson. We would stop at the park just over the railroad tracks where there was a monument with all the names of the people from Delanson, who had served and died in World Wars I and II. Someone would play "Taps" and three or four uniformed servicemen would fire their rifles three times in honor of the brave men who had fought and died for our freedom. Next, we would regroup and parade up the hill into Grove Cemetery and wait for someone to say a dedication or prayer over the cemetery in honor of that day. Then we marched out of the cemetery down the hill, back up to the high school, and that was it for the year as a marching band. At that time, the cemetery had no meaning for me. Many people were buried there; people Mom had known, and people I knew when I was a young girl. On those Memorial Days, I only paid attention to which boys noticed me and how I would fit in with the rest of the day's events.

CHAPTER TWENTY-FOUR

Leaving The Sofa

I SPENT TIME WITH WILL, THE HIGH SCHOOL FRIEND WITH WHOM I reconnected. We met mostly later in the afternoon when either Denise or Diana took over at the condo. By then, we had realized Mom and Dad could not be left alone for very long. Dad had only one evening out, which was Thursdays. At 8 p.m., he went down to the game room at the condo for Poker Night. That came to an abrupt end when someone came into the game room to tell Dad that Mom was in her wheelchair in the hallway outside of their condo, crying and calling for him.

At this point, Mom was struggling to remain mobile while her body became heavier with a fluid buildup and most attempts to do what had always been normal for her ceased. During the middle of another night, Mom got up, forgetting that she was not able to do so easily and fell onto their kitchen floor. They called Denise and Paul, who came over within ten minutes. Meanwhile, Dad called hospice at their 24-hour call center. They put him on hold and didn't pick up again. After complaining to the Saratoga Hospice supervisor, they investigated the incident. After that, they apologized each time they saw us.

It showed me how overwhelmed this system of hospice care is. There are not enough nurses, social workers or volunteers to care for the thousands in great need on a daily basis. I selfishly assumed that we would have much more assistance for much longer.

As Mom's condition deteriorated, and morphine was introduced into her care, our levels of stress mounted.

Katherine came to be with her grandmother for a week before leaving on a trip to Lyon, France. Katherine and Mom had an interesting relationship. Not really close, not as close as Mom and Chetty's, but they had fun together through the years. Katherine had always been stubborn and stood up for herself, which made me happy and proud. Mom and Dad had no idea what to do with her.

On one of my parents' visits to us when Katherine was about seven, they were babysitting and experienced her strong personality firsthand. Katherine had wanted to walk over to our neighbor's house to visit her friend. Dad told her no, so Katherine put her coat on, opened the door and went anyway.

Both of our children were raised Catholic, as Chet and I had been. Saints John and Paul in Wexford, Pennsylvania, was a new parish at that time begun by Father Dan Dinardo. He is now Cardinal Dinardo in Rome. In the early 1990s, parishioners were redistricted from three churches in this area of Southwestern Pennsylvania and Father Dinardo led us to become one of the largest, most active parishes in the area. Boy, was it ever growing by leaps and bounds, the very same reason we had moved there to begin our business. The closeness of church members in the beginning created an environment of family and great support for those not originally from the area, especially for those of us with very young children. Both Chetty and Katherine were baptized, celebrated their first communions and were confirmed at this church.

Katherine went to Mercyhurst University in Erie, Pennsylvania, and was in her sophomore year at the time. While attending Mercyhurst, she had begun her exploration of spirituality. With the openness that so characterizes her wonderful personality, Katherine decided to become Wiccan. She shared this with Mom in the hope of getting her blessing about moving on from Catholicism to this new way of faith.

Mom was still in a relatively coherent state of mind at this point. Katherine was sitting on the sofa with Mom with the intention of sharing something very important with her. I was sitting nearby but not in their space. While Katherine calmly shared all of her information, I looked on. Mom smiled and told Katherine she approved of whatever she felt was right for her. I kept my inner exclamations of "Where is all of this wonderfulness coming from and why did it take so long?" to myself. It was so amazing to see this very important moment for both of them.

It especially surprised me since this was on the same day that Katherine had caught Mom telling a fib about weighing herself and tattled on her to the hospice workers.

I must admit there is a part of my mother's spirit which resides within Katherine... the will to do what she needs to do in order to survive and remain true to her inner self. I wouldn't be surprised if both Katherine and I find comfort one day while we are lying on our right sides on the left corners of our sofas.

Mom was very loving and kind as her days were coming to an end. I was entering a time, I realized, that was a beautiful reminder of our earliest days together. I treasured the times that Dad, Mom and I were alone. We spoke about those times that no one knew about, but us: mostly days spent with my own Grandma Cecelia, either picnicking in the Adirondacks or spending long, wonderful Sundays at the farm with aunts, uncles, and cousins. They smiled. Dad was tearful. I held it together as those days were brought back to mind for all of us.

Around my third week at Mom and Dad's, hospice suggested we begin giving Mom morphine by mouth. This was difficult as Mom held her mouth shut and refused it. The hospice nurses were unable to care for her properly due to the position she was in on the sofa, so they tried to coax her into her hospital bed. They didn't understand why she wouldn't get into it so they could help her. These were end-of-life procedures like inserting a catheter and turning her from side to side. Mom would have none of it, even though the sores on her elbows were obviously painful. She would lean on her elbow on the arm of the sofa, slump down, then pull herself up and fall asleep. She did that all day and all night long. There was no other way she could get comfortable. After a few days, we vowed the next time she woke up, we were getting her into that hospital bed or at least, have her switch to lying on her left side on the right corner of the sofa.

When she woke up, she was very groggy from the morphine, so I was able to coax her up into a sitting position. She seemed okay with that but was unable to stay upright for long. As I attempted to get her to lie down on her left side, she flailed about like she was falling off a cliff. She panicked, begging to be on her other side. She didn't care about the sores or what the nurses couldn't do. She really couldn't cope with the change we were trying to impose on her, even if it was for her comfort. We began to realize how that position in the small place on the sofa had always been her only safe place, ever. It was the only spot in the world where she knew she was going to be okay.

Sometimes, I would get into the hospital bed myself in an attempt to show her how much fun it was. It reminded me of how I tried to show her, all those years ago, how much fun driving could be. Here we were, many years later, and still my cajoling and antics accomplished nothing. There would be no hospital bed for her. She just smiled and floated off into some other place and time.

One of the most poignant scenes I remember was when her hands and fingers showed signs of swelling and her wedding rings and class ring were too tight, cutting off the circulation to her fingers. As Mom looked on with no emotion or comment, Denise lovingly took some warm soap and water and gently removed her engagement ring and wedding band from her left hand. Watching that being done to her shook us all to the core. She hadn't taken her rings off for over 55 years. Dad was in the background, tearful and unable to come any closer.

Denise was cute with Mom and said, "There, all done," as if she were a small child. Mom seemed not to be bothered by it for when it was over, she simply sat back into her safe place on the sofa. We placed all her rings in her jewelry box for safe keeping. Denise stepped out onto the small balcony off the living room and closed the glass sliding door behind her, spending some time on her own. Removing Mom's rings, I imagine, had taken a toll on Denise, possibly more than anything else she had done for her. And, Denise had done a great deal.

The next day, the hospice nurse demanded that Mom get into the hospital bed, as they couldn't care for her the way they needed to. Mom refused, being irritated and even more determined to force her elbow and upper arm to remain in place leaning on that arm of the sofa. Her sores were bleeding now. We put Band-Aids over the bleeding sores and packed pillows around her to make her comfortable.

Kathy, the hospice worker who was now visiting us on a daily basis, had a serious talk with us. She said we needed to get Mom into the bed because they had her on diuretics, and her kidneys were no longer working. She needed a catheter that very day.

On that fateful day of reckoning, Kathy and I were alone with Mom and told her it was time to get into the hospital bed. She began to go into a panic and said "No." I got onto the bed assisting Kathy in an attempt to get Mom to, at least, sit on it. She flailed her arms as if she was fighting for her life. She couldn't stand up on her own, and as Kathy struggled to get her upright, it seemed as though Kathy was about to lose the little patience she had left. I began a familiar cadence with Mom as I had done so many times before.

"Mom, look at me," I said firmly. She turned her head, and I held her eyes with mine and gently guided her into place with as loving and encouraging words as possible. She finally relented, and Kathy and I no longer had a fight on our hands. With the awkwardness of both of us attempting to position Mom so her head was raised on the lifted top of the bed, we were exhausted, especially Mom. She fell to sleep at once.

Kathy looked at me and said, "You did a great job with her. That was difficult." I wasn't sure if it was difficult, maybe it was. It was definitely familiar.

Once we settled her into that hospital bed as best we could, I took a break and left for the rest of the afternoon. At this point, we all were taking turns doing the morning and early afternoon shift with my parents. Eventually, we added an evening overnight shift. I mostly took that shift as the twins and Dina needed to tend to their homes and families. I was on my own and had dedicated whatever time it took to remain in Clifton Park. I was lucky to be able to take time off to do so. My clients were tolerant of this four-week break. Some needed phone sessions, which seemed to get them through during our time spent apart.

On one of my day shifts, I left the condo for a break. My son, Chet, and Diana stayed to spend time with Mom and Dad. We were increasing Mom's anti-anxiety medicine and morphine as her agitated state of being in that bed demanded it.

There is something called "the surge," where some patients near death have a sudden burst of clarity and strength, both physically and mentally. Later on that day, Mom had hers. Chet, who was stationed at Ft. Sam Houston, had flown up to see Mom. Chet had spent time with his grandma a few days before she entered the inner sanctum of the hell that was the hospital bed. He had fun with Grandma and Grandpa, as he always had. Chet is funny, and his personality has always been what people need to feel better. Chet was their first grandson, and the three of them have a special bond.

Diana told us things had seemed to be going well. Chet was standing on one side of Mom's bed and Diana on the other, just talking, when all of a sudden Mom tried to jump out of the bed. It seemed Mom was headed in the direction of the sliding glass doors out to the balcony. Diana said it was like fighting a tiger to get her back sitting upright on the bed. In doing so, Mom was left in an awkward and dangerous position, leaning way over the metal arm of the left side of the bed about to fall out. They were both afraid of the catheter coming out since the hospice workers wouldn't be back until morning.

Mom was now in survival mode. With everything the hospital bed meant to her, she was fighting for her life, or at least fighting to get back to the sofa. Both Diana and Chet struggled to pull Mom's body, which was heavy now without any way to stop the buildup of fluids, into an upright position.

Finally, Chet was able to put a move on Mom that he had learned in a section of his active duty called Combatives. He scooped Mom up with both his arms locked in her underarm area and got her back into place. We later joked that Chet had put a choke hold on Grandma. Once that was accomplished, she went into a deep sleep from which she did not return, except for a brief "Goodbye" on the night before she passed away.

CHAPTER TWENTY-FIVE

Making It Okay To Let Go

ON SATURDAY MORNING, THE NURSE TOLD US SHE DIDN'T THINK MOM would make it through the evening. We had visitors come in and out throughout that day, mostly all of the brothers- and sisters-in-law about whom she had always talked negatively and claimed she hated. It was so bizarre to see everyone come into the condo and see us kids and Dad surrounding her bed. We were tending to her and looking up briefly to nod a hello. Then we would wipe or caress her face, hoping she would open her eyes, look at us and say something more.

We called the priest, the one Mom thought had fallen in love with her, and asked him to come as soon as possible and say prayers with us around her bed.

Most of that day was the deathbed vigil. I held Mom's tiny feet. She had the most beautiful, tiny, doll-like feet. They were still pink and looked healthy. The twins kept busy talking to whoever came in to be with us and called the White-Van Buren Funeral home in Delanson to begin the process of whatever was to happen after Mom passed away.

All the words said seemed as though they were about someone other than Mom. It wasn't real, wasn't happening. But, it was. Denise and Diana were good at doing the planning and coordinating of what would come next.

Early that evening, the priest came up to the condo to give Mom last rites and pray with us. He came into the living room and stood by Mom's side, holding her hand and making the official motions priests make for Catholics near death. We had asked Dina and her son, Tyler, to come over to pray with us. Dad, Denise, Diana, Dave, the priest and I were holding hands as Dina and Tyler came in the door. Dina was totally shocked. When she had last seen her, Mom was still talking and doing fairly well. Now, we were all tearfully holding hands about to say our goodbyes. We began using the words we had learned in early Sunday school and in our childhood evening prayers when Mom had knelt with us by our beds. My Aunt Noreen, Uncle Floyd, Uncle Leon, Aunt Bev and several others who had lived and celebrated and struggled together with my parents for over 70 years were now at the bedside. Mom was the first of them to die. All my Dad's siblings were alive as were their spouses.

The priest led us in the Our Father, Hail Mary, and Glory Be. Mom's only participation was the sound of her breathing pattern becoming more of a struggle as her lungs were no longer working. Then, we all said goodbye to the priest. The relatives hugged and kissed us and left for a healthier, happier surrounding than that in which we were to remain. Lucky them!

Earlier in the week, the twins, Dina and I had gone to dinner and talked about whether there would come a time when we would be telling Mom it would be okay to let go. At that time, no one could imagine doing it; it was just a thought. The hospital bed was in the center of the living room, close to the sliding glass doors Mom had attempted to reach. After everyone left, Dave wanted to cook and spent a great deal of time making Chicken Picatta while we all talked and walked around as if at a party.

We all took turns going over to Mom, making our silent prayers or pleas for her not to struggle like this anymore. She wasn't in any obvious pain other than very labored and raspy-sounding breathing.

After dinner, we all sat around and watched Mom. Dishes were done, and things put away. Dave now stood at the head of Mom's bed stroking her hair softly telling her how much he loved her and hoping she knew he was there. Mom's "sofa," now a safe distance from the hospital bed, was the perfect location for Denise, Diana and Dina to hold their vigil. Denise sat on the left side, Diana in the middle and Dina on the right. I was sitting on the floor, my favorite spot, and Dad continued to cry and pace. How sad and bonding this night was for us. The atmosphere was solemn. No one said a word until Denise leaned over, looking at the rest of us, and said, "Maybe someone should go up and say something to Mom."

I was looking at Mom's bed, and when I turned to look back at my sisters, they all had their pointer fingers touching the end of their noses. We used to do this as a sign when playing a card game or any game to signal we were "not it." The thing is I didn't realize, at a time like this, we would be playing by those rules. It was so funny to see them all with fingers on their noses. They were definitely not in the running for this particular part of the game. I looked at them and said, "What are you guys doing?" They were all laughing and sitting as far back as they could on the sofa. They would've all been sitting on the kitchen counter if they could have as it was farther from Mom's bed.

There was comic relief in those brief moments. They found a way to deal with the pain through humor and the shift from the heaviness of the grief was what we all needed.

Dave paid no attention to what was happening. I got up reluctantly and said, "Okay, fine, but this is not fair. You didn't give me a chance to vote!"

I walked over to Mom's hospital bed knowing, deep in my heart, that I needed to be the one doing this. I looked at Dad's exhausted, sad face showing no signs of being aware of what was going on. So, I approached Mom's bed and felt the urge to get up and be close to her when I shared whatever words were about to come out. I climbed onto her bed, nestled in as close as I could, holding the parts of the blanket that covered her body, leaned in and said, "Mom, it's okay. Everything's going to be okay. You can let go and not struggle anymore."

With that came a sound none of us had heard before, like a gurgling puff of bubbles from Mom that seemed to me like she was struggling even more. I immediately leaned even closer to Mom, attempting to do what I had always done to reassure her that she was going to be okay. "It's okay, Mom, I love you; we all love you. Dad's going to be fine. We will all be okay. You can let go."

Mom made a loud grunt that shocked all of us. Still leaning up close to Mom's face, I looked up at Dave, who still stroked her hair and said, "Did you hear that?" He looked down at me with a tearful wide-eyed smile and nodded, yes. I leaned back up on my knees and said, "Or not, Mom, that's okay. You do whatever you need to do."

That was the last communication from my mother to me and the world. My mother remained unchanged to the very end. Why I thought I could tell her to do anything was beyond me.

I got off the bed and went over to the floor where I had been sitting before. I felt strangely embarrassed for trying to be so loving towards her and only receiving a rebuff, a rejection. Dina looked at me and said, "It seemed like Mom said, 'No, and get off the bed.' Leave it to our mother to ruin an emotional moment." Shaking my head, I sat there and started to giggle. We all did because that was how she was. What I did by trying to be dramatic and overly sensitive to her every need was how I was. Both of us stayed true to each other until the end. We were the way we had always been. Denise leaned over from the end of the sofa and said to me, "You had to say it twice? How funny!"

By that time, we were all emotionally spent. I left to go to Will's for the evening and everyone, except for Dave and Dad, left to go their separate ways. Chet had left a few days before as he had to return to his Army duty and Katherine had gone back to France. She felt comfortable leaving as Mom had urged her to go abroad.

I drove to Will's house and was glad he was there to hold me. He was dark, handsome and very kind. At this time, I needed him to be. We fell asleep around 11 p.m.

Dave called me at 3:30 a.m. and said, "Mom stopped breathing."

"It's okay, Dave," I said. "I'll be right there."

Will and I held each other for a short while before I got up and dressed in the clothing I had dropped by the bed. Then I went down to my car and sat there for a minute making sure I was all right to drive. I felt strangely okay and began the short drive back to the condo.

It was dark, and there was a soft, steady rain. I couldn't believe Mom was gone though I didn't know if a doctor or hospice nurse had come out to say she was. As I drove past a 24-hour McDonalds, I was furious that anyone could be doing anything as normal as going in there. My mom had just died. None of it made sense; yet, all of it fit into place as what was supposed to be happening.

I parked outside the condo complex, near the front lobby, so I could walk in the front doors without bothering anyone to toss down the keys. The ride up in the elevator this time was different than all of the other times. I was preparing in a different way. So many questions came to me. How would she look? How would she be? Were the twins and Dina there yet or just Dave and Dad? How were we all going to handle this next part?

CHAPTER TWENTY-SIX

Our Hospice Angel

DENISE TOLD ME THAT ROB FROM THE WHITE-VAN BUREN FUNERAL Home had instructed her to call them after Mom had passed, and they would come out from Delanson to take care of her from there. Calm and organized, Denise and Diana had things in place as to how to proceed from here. Also, Denise said the hospice workers had told her to call them as soon as Mom passed so a nurse could come to officially pronounce her death and get her ready to leave.

When I arrived, Diana, Denise and Paul had already gotten there. Dave was standing by Mom's bedside and Dad was wandering around lost. We were all a bit lost now that our focus and actions no longer centered around keeping Mom alive and comfortable. Dinner the night before had been an attempt at normality in spite of the fact our mother lay dying in front of us in that damn hospital bed.

No one from hospice was there yet, just us. I looked at Mom. She seemed peaceful, finally, without anxiety and the pain she had endured in her life. She was now on her way to wherever this next part would take her, and for the first time in my life, I was not a part of where she was.

Denise was cleaning and was emphatic that we would be getting rid of that damn sofa as soon as possible. It was covered with towels and blankets. All the germs Mom had left behind meant we would need to get rid of it as soon as possible. I would have taken that sofa with me, if I could.

The twins and Denise's husband, Paul, were leaning on the kitchen counter, talking about the next steps. Denise stepped away from the kitchen counter from time to time with Febreze in hand and the vacuum ready.

Denise and Diana had faithfully come each week to clean for Mom and Dad, while Dina cooked and baked, making the drive of more than an hour each way from Tribes Hill.

On this day, the place looked spotless. The only clutter was on the small wooden table separating the kitchen and living room. Several full bottles of morphine, notes of Dave's flight information, and a report from Dad's recent trip to the ER were on the table. There was also information from hospice on what to expect when your loved one is dying.

Dina didn't come back that morning. I don't blame her. It was very difficult to be with Mom's dead body lying there with nothing else we could do for her. Nothing more.

Donna, a hospice nurse arrived to watch over Mom's body so nothing would happen to it. She was in her early 30s, kind and comforting as she picked up the pace for us on what was to be done next. Donna went to Mom and told us how wonderful she looked, emphasizing that we had done a great job taking care of her. Donna said Mom reminded her of her mother.

"Your mom looks so sweet!" she said as she went about her preparations to get Mom cleaned and dressed.

From the sofa, I watched as she took Mom's pulse from several areas on her body and pronounced that she had, indeed, passed away. It was now around 5 a.m., but by the feel and look of Mom, Donna pronounced her death as 4 a.m.

Donna asked if anyone would mind helping her take care of Mom. No one moved or said anything. After a pause, I said, "I will." The twins were busy picking up around the condo and selecting clothes in which Donna would dress Mom. Denise brought out a sundress which Donna pronounced as being so "sweet." She asked me to hold up the blue blanket, covering Mom as she carefully did her work and spoke comfortingly all the while. She wanted to know which sister I was and if there was anything else I wanted to share about myself with her.

"Your Mom is lucky to have such a beautiful family," she said. "Many times, when I come to do this, the family members are distraught and unable to handle the reality of their loved one's death. There is often chaos and drama filling the room."

I continued to hold up the blue blanket while Donna finished taking care of the beautiful cleansing of the body that is a part of all cultures around the world. It was now our turn to experience this rite of passage.

Once Donna had finished, she asked for the dress we had chosen for Mom. We were, at last, with someone who was gentle and loving, guiding us through how to do this beautiful/horrible aspect of Mom's transition. There was a sense of confidence for all of us that we could now let go.

I held up the blanket for just a bit longer as Donna dressed Mom in a smooth, easy way that showed she was meant to do this work. This short partnership of Donna and me was finished. Mom was dressed and ready to go. Rob, the coroner, had already come in during this time, but I hadn't even noticed because I was so involved with what Donna and I were doing.

"It's probably best that you all head into another room for this part," Rob suggested as he wheeled the gurney in. "We will be taking your mom now." Paul had left by then. The rest of us said our good-byes to Mom and filed into Dad's bedroom.

I hesitated. Denise opened Dad's bedroom door. Neither of us could resist taking one last peek even though we had no idea of what we would see. She and I watched Mom being wheeled out of the living room by one of the men from the funeral home. I seem to remember Denise walking away from the door, but I kept watching, mesmerized by this strangely beautiful last sight.

Mom was in a black body bag with only her face showing. She would have wanted it that way, not zipped up in that claustrophobia-inducing bag, but with her face exposed, saying goodbye. A burgundy colored blanket was surrounding her. My breath caught in my throat as I realized how beautiful she was and that she was, indeed, going to be okay.

We stayed in Dad's bedroom for a while, comforting Dad. He had been talking to Donna from time to time as the men from the funeral home were doing their work. Dad kept repeating how lucky they were to have us kids to help. Donna was still in the living room gathering her things and taking care of last minute tasks before she left.

When we opened the bedroom door into the living room, Mom was gone, and Donna was not there either. She had made up the hospital bed and placed the wooden angel that I had given Mom when I first arrived on the pillow.

We were trying to make sense of what had happened and decided to go for coffee or breakfast somewhere. There's the best diner in Mechanicville, Bubbles, about 15 minutes down the road. We had gone there from time to time throughout these last four weeks and decided to go there now.

In a confused, strange haze, we gathered our things and were preparing to leave when we realized Donna was at the door waiting to say goodbye, which she did to each and every one of us. It was as though she was a member of the family who had come to carry us through one of the hardest parts of our lives. She was smiling and giggling a little as she kissed and hugged each of us, saying something meaningful. She said how lucky she felt to have met each one of us and what memories she would take with her. It was like a receiving line she was going down, connecting to show us how special we all were to her.

I was at the end of the line. With tears in both of our eyes, we hugged in a way that solidified the bond we had made. Donna kept her arms around me, leaned back a bit, looked me straight in the eyes and said, "Tin Man, I think I'm going to miss you most of all."

And with that, I finally heard what I had always wanted to hear. From a stranger, there was validation of the kind I needed. I really was a good person. Like the Tin Man character in *The Wizard of Oz*, I was the most tender and emotional of all. Approval, at last.

I haven't ever seen Donna again. We met for only an hour or so at a moment in my life which was one of the most memorable. Donna saw what I had hoped Mom and Dad or anyone in my family would see…that I loved them, especially Mom. There was no shame in it. Staying open to opportunity, and saying yes to helping Donna clean and prepare Mom after her death seemed to fulfill the cycle of the relationship I had with Mom from my birth until her death. Donna looked me directly in the eyes when she made the Tin Man comment and I knew I was going to be okay.

That took my breath away. The validation and recognition that I so yearned for throughout my life, and especially in Mom's last days, was gifted to me through this angel sent to guide us through our darkest hours.

CHAPTER TWENTY-SEVEN

Where Is She Really?

I DROVE TO BUBBLES IN THE NUMB STATE THAT NATURE GIVES US AS an illusion of well-being in the moments and days after the loss of a loved one. We looked back…only ten minutes after leaving the condo, wondering how we were able to say and do the things we did in those moments by Mom's side. There is a loss that goes on and on without end. I had begun my journey without Mom in my life, now a motherless daughter, as Hope Edelman describes so poignantly in her book, *Motherless Daughters.*

What the weather was like, all the sights of that morning, rainy but clearing up as the morning progressed, remain with me still.

Once inside Bubbles, the smells of breakfast and the sound of people on a Sunday morning all doing their normal Sunday routine surrounded us. We sat down, began talking and drinking coffee as if nothing major had just occurred. My journey of eating my way through the early days of my mother's death began right then, right there in that restaurant with lots of coffee and a huge piece of choc-olate cake with white icing. The best there is.

Later, we gathered at Denise's house to talk more about Mom's funeral arrangements. Denise and Diana took charge, thankfully, of where, when and with whom the service and burial would take place. The twins had been in contact with the White-Van Buren Funeral Home a week or so before and were taking care of this part as if they had done it before. Mom wanted to be cremated and only have a small, short memorial service before being buried in a small plot in Grove Cemetery reserved for those who were cremated.

On this day, July 29th, still the same day that Mom died, we were at Denise's house going through photos of Mom as a little girl. There were not many of those. There were a few high school photos, many of her after she was married, and with us kids and then grandkids. Diana took over the responsibility of writing the obituary for the newspaper. All of these things I couldn't and didn't get into. I couldn't think clearly enough to write an obituary or to be organized at all, for that matter. I offered help, but this type of planning and organizing was where Denise and Diana excelled, and they did a beautiful job.

Mom's service was the following Wednesday from 9 a.m. to 12 noon. Honestly, I think we all thought that only a few people would attend. I always imagined that Mom had burned so many bridges with family and friends that many people would choose not to attend.

We gathered, again at Denise and Paul's home to look through more photos and greet relatives who came from Long Island (Tommy, Mom's oldest brother), Plattsburgh (Philly, Mom's foster sister) and others from Pittsburgh.

I made regular trips to Bubbles for cake and, eventually, bought a huge chocolate cake with white icing to take to Denise's so I would have my handy supply. She and Paul had built a beautiful home that was always spotless. I consistently had a glass of ice water with me and tried not to spill or make watermarks on their expensive, handsome furniture.

At night, to try to sleep, we retreated to Diana's beautiful center hall colonial, which she and John had built in Burnt Hills. Dave remained with Dad at the condo, going through some of Mom's things to see what remembrances of Mom could be given to the grandchildren.

Mom had very little jewelry (her engagement and wedding rings and a high school class ring.) She was not into buying things for herself, ever. She carefully managed the household budget and made sure, most importantly, that Dad had a $20.00 per week allowance. There was always fighting about that as Dad had to ask her for money, but she ruled in that way, thank God. Most of her energy in the years when we were growing up, and even later, went into building a home, making sure her husband and children were fed and clothed.

During the most difficult of years when the kids were little and before Dina was born, bill collectors often came knocking at the main wooden front door that no one else ever used. It was a signal for Mom and me to hide the kids behind the sofa and make a game out of who could be the quietest. One day I watched from our front bay window as a tow truck backed into our driveway. A man got out and chained the only car we had to his truck. Then, he towed it away. Dad had not made the payments so the car was repossessed.

Soon after this, they were barely able to save the house from going the way of the car. Eventually, they were able to get a used vehicle. Mom was able to keep our family together in the only way she knew how.

She told me years later that she knew when going into the marriage that she would face hardship because of Dad's relationship with money. Dad borrowed money from Aunt Rose to buy her engagement ring and conveniently forgot to repay Aunt Rose whether on purpose or some rationalization or justification of his own. So, Mom paid the money back.

> Often there are warning signs of possible problems when we marry, but we marry anyway. The whole idea of denial, blaming and secrecy has to do with more than addiction. It is a tried and true coping mechanism for times when we want what we want when we want it and will figure out how to handle the consequences later.

CHAPTER TWENTY-EIGHT

Through The Eyes of Others

THE RITUAL THAT MOM AND DAD HAD OF CRITICIZING AND JUDGING everyone, including us kids and our families went on until Mom could no longer speak. Every evening, they would bring up someone who had either bothered them or done some perceived wrong to them. Then, they would spend time before going to bed determining why this person or these people were no good or emotionally unbalanced. When both of them felt they were in a place above all the others, they could go to bed assured they were going to be okay. They had determined they were not like the other people in the world they had just cancelled out. This had gone on all my years growing up, a habit that was confusing and became tempting to do. I found judging others to be one of the hardest traits of mine of which to let go. This habit is a bad one!

Because of Mom and Dad's thinly veiled attempts to judge everyone in their world, we couldn't imagine many people would come to the memorial service. The family members all arrived about the same time. Will and his daughter, Kylie, drove with me and were an amazing support. Will said it was just the right thing to do. I appreciated it.

Denise and Diana (mostly Denise) had planned a short service with a word from the local priest at the end. The White-Van Buren Funeral Home is somewhat small with room for a general flow of people if a large crowd is anticipated. We didn't anticipate some family members coming, but to our surprise, over 175 people came to pay their respects and show their support to Dad and our family. It was a very hot day in July and it felt as if there was no air conditioning.

We gathered around a table where Mom's ashes were in a beautiful urn with a lovely flower arrangement surrounding it. We had deliberately chosen a small arrangement, instead of one that would overwhelm as we didn't want it to take away from the attention to Mom's place of being.

The more crowded the room became, the more I could feel my claustrophobia and panic set in. There were so many people who knew my parents from their younger school days and people who had recently met us…even my new friend, Bob, from the 12 Step Recovery meetings I attended each day.

The ones who were noticeably not in attendance were my former in-laws whom everyone asked about. They didn't send a card, flowers, nor did they even make a phone call, not any of them. I felt embarrassed for them and finally saw what I had been blind to for years. The others not in attendance were the actual relatives of Aunt Rose. Mom's sister, Maggie, came to the funeral home as well as Uncle Tom. Many of my beloved cousins, from both sides of our family, attended the memorial service. It's interesting how we noticed who wasn't there as much as we noticed who did make the effort to come all the way out to Delanson.

The crowd exceeded the number of chairs the funeral home had set out and trickled out the door to the road. I was surprised to hear from many of the people who came to Mom's memorial service just how much Mom had meant to them. I think maybe it was by being herself that she had given honestly to others and people appreciated her authenticity.

The day before, my sisters asked me to say something at the viewing. Of course, I loved the idea. I had thought of some things to say, mostly about how dedicated we siblings were to taking care of Mom and each other. The words came from a familiar place within.

"On behalf of my father, sisters, and brother, I thank you all for coming to be with us today. It means a great deal..."

Putting humor into anything I say seems to be automatic. I thought about saying, "Since we thought no one would be here," but I didn't. I did, however, share with them two funny stories.

"Mom told us about when she first met Dad in seventh grade. The story goes that Mom loved Dad from the minute she set eyes on him and at that time she told her friend, Betty Jean Snyder, that she was going to marry him. She was twelve. Mom said she went up to Dad to tell him she liked him, and he punched her. The next day, he brought her a calendar. They became friends, but they didn't start serious dating until they were in their junior year of high school."

Dad, sitting in the front row, stated that every time she told that story, he never had any idea what she was talking about. There was laughter from the crowd. I love an audience. I was on a roll and let it rip.

I shared one more story. I wondered if it was a good idea, but I had to. I told of the recent events of my attempting to tell my mother she could "die already." I put into plain words for this crowd of mourners, one of the most dramatic moments of my life. I shared how I had leaned over and whispered loving words of saying goodbye and telling Mom it was okay for her to let go. I described how Mom looking frustrated even in her coma, simply grunted her message loud and clear, "No." Everyone thought it was going to be a tender last moment with my mother but it turned their tears into peals of laughter. Anyone who knew Mom could envision the moment clearly. No one was going to tell my mother anything. It was my way of sharing with everyone, in a funny down to earth way, how much she meant to us.

We drove up to the Grove Cemetery for the graveside service. Once there, I took a few minutes to look around at the familiar names on the headstones of friends and relatives I knew or had heard about through the countless stories Mom had told us. This experience reminded me of the classic play by Thorton Wilder called *Our Town*. The third act of *Our Town* shows an empty stage except for three rows of chairs representing gravestones. The *Our Town* cemetery overlooks the town below, as does Grove Cemetery overlook the town of Delanson. In the play, those who have passed away sit serenely on their chairs looking out at the people who are standing, crying at the gravesites. The stage manager who narrates most of the play in *Our Town* tells us, "People live and die and time marches on. There's something way down deep that's eternal about every human being."

Looking at so many of the names on these graves brought waves of memories and made me think of them as though they were all alive not that long ago.

CHAPTER TWENTY-NINE

Mom's Legacy

ONCE I BECAME SOBER, I BEGAN ACTING AND DANCING AGAIN. NOW, for the first time with this book, I have put pen to paper. This book is my way of sharing all of what Mom meant to me. It is not about what she didn't do or say. It's about what she did give to us...me especially. She gave us more than we ever imagined or acknowledged. She was an abandoned little three-year-old girl who lived the rest of her life knowing her mother didn't want her and left her. I didn't have that experience. I had a mother. She didn't leave us, even during those very difficult years.

More than that, she gave us stories she made up when we were little. She loved it when it stormed outside, especially thunder and lightning. It was fun for her as she remembered Aunt Rose and all of the relatives coming downstairs to say the rosary under the dining room table when it stormed. Mom didn't want us to have that "nonsense," as she called it, for memories. She was a fighter, as she proved on her last day of life. She was going to go out on her terms doing it the way she wanted.

When I became a therapist, I realized how great it was that Mom was able to stand up for herself and not let others, especially Dad, walk all over her. She was a great role model for how to set boundaries.

Mom once told me that when she gave birth to me, the first thing she said when she saw me was, "How could my mother leave me?" In her way, she left a legacy of love beyond understanding. It was not the way I wanted her to demonstrate her love, but it was the mothering I needed to be exactly who I am today and, for that, I am eternally grateful.

In the years since the death of my mother, I have discovered daily the courage and bravery it takes to allow myself to grieve out loud. There is no such thing as "anticipatory grief." The feelings we have before our loved one passes away don't prepare us for the actual grief that comes after our loved one has died. There is no way we can prepare. Death brings an entire range of emotions we have never felt before. Due to the incredible pain we feel with any loss, many of us will drink, drug, sex, eat or not eat, spend, or gamble our grief away. It would be great if anything I felt before she died took away the pain that came after her death. The phrase "anticipatory grief" makes as much sense as "anticipatory birth." There may be expectations on how to mother the child soon to be born, yet, any of those thoughts or feelings of "anticipation" may be very difficult to remember after that birth.

The relationship with a newborn is unique with each participant. It takes days, weeks and years to develop a relationship with this new, unique individual as his or her mother, father, sibling, friend, and so on, throughout that individual's life. So it is when that individual passes away. The period should be given as much time or more to adjust to what is now as new to us as when that person was first born. The beauty and respect that society allows us as the mother to a newborn should be equal to what is allowed in our period of grief through the loss of our loved one. Instead of walking one day at a time with my mom, as I did from the beginning, I now walk through the rest of my life, one day at a time, without her.

The first few days after the memorial service, we wandered around each other as we got ready to fly back, drive back or somehow get back to our previous lives. Those of us who were masters at keeping busy continued. Diana told us that on the day Mom died, she had done seven loads of laundry. The twins had cleaned the condo for Dad on that day and continue to do so every week.

To hear myself say, "My mother died" comes from a place within, which is foreign to me still. I continue to ask, "I know she died, but where is she really?" That plea is often met with blank stares, but sometimes, I am with someone who gets it. How can I be motherless?

Research suggests we don't begin the true grieving process until about six months after our loved one's death. The "firsts" of that year include the first holidays without them, the first anniversaries, the change of seasons (summer, fall, winter, spring), as well as smells, sights, sounds, touches and tastes. Whenever I experience any of these things, I have waves of emotion so intense there is nothing I can do other than let them come.

The idea that the lifelong relationship with our loved one can be grieved away in an allotted amount of time is ludicrous. There is no such thing as being finished with our grieving or getting over a loss. It becomes...different with time.

Being a member of the club to which no one wants to belong, the Grief Club, I have realized the need to go through and not around my feelings. There is also what I call "the slinky effect" where it seems like former unresolved losses come and bounce on my shoulders... like the rings of a slinky one on top of the other.

Not talking about the loss of a loved one, in some cases, ever again, can create a growing disconnection within ourselves. Grief waits. When we try to "get rid" of deep waves of longing in a way that used to sooth or numb us, we find it's not enough. If we need more of whatever it is more often, my hope is for us to find a way through grieving in rooms of support for and with each other and not in silence.

When we have unsuccessful attempts at "moving on" from our grief, we develop a subtle but perceptible shift in personality and that impacts the people around us. Again, grief waits.

We can be masters at keeping too busy to do the emotional work to heal, even for extended periods of time. Healing comes when we share with each other openly and honestly. Healing begins when we are heard and understood by someone who listens, without saying well-meaning cliché's. Grief is a beautiful, horrible thing. How we grieve will make a difference, an impact, on those around us and on generations to come.

The most difficult day of that first year without Mom was my birthday. Mom always made a big deal over our birthdays. If there was ever a time when she showed us that we were special to her, it was on our birthdays. How could I have a birthday without her?

I am who I am because Mom gave of herself from the moment I was born until she died, in the only way she knew how. Selfishly, I can now say I am grateful to have been the firstborn and to have had my first six years alone with her. It's not what she didn't do or didn't say or didn't give me, but what she did. She didn't take my hand and walk me down to someone else's house to give me away. She held my hand until I let go of hers.

I am okay!

Epilogue

I'M NOT EXACTLY SURE WHEN MY CONFUSION AND DREAD SHIFTED to confidence and understanding of myself. What I am clearly aware of was my absolute need to face my fears and "do it anyway"…whatever "it" was at the time. I made many "mistakes" which were beautiful opportunities to have been kinder to myself as I sought my way through the "how" of it.

My first three years as a counselor, right out of Graduate school, I worked in the Detox Unit at Gateway Rehabilitation Center along side nationally renown psychiatrist Dr. Neil Capretto from whom I gained enormous insight into the world of addiction. This is one of my favorite places to have worked. In Detox, I preferred working in the Men's wing. When I spent time working with females, they were nasty, manipulative and would take every opportunity to cause trouble. I had to spend an enormous amount of time clarifying to my superiors what my actual conversations with them were because they twisted the meaning and intention of my words to serve their own purposes. And that was exhausting!

The men wanted to be left alone and when asked questions, all they wanted to do was deck you. Since that never happened, it was no big deal to me. They are angry and filled with rage. The aim of my work in Detox through individual sessions and group therapy was to allow patients to know the reality of how they truly felt underneath all of the anger. Hiding under that anger is fear and sadness. I wanted to take my patients to the raw and vulnerable places from which they had been hiding. The common cry of every human about to drink or drug themselves to death is, "I don't care."

I left the Detox Unit and spent a year working as a therapist at Western Psychiatric Institute and Clinic in the city of Pittsburgh. I encountered a facility struggling to move the masses of mentally ill patients through the mental health care system. Keeping strict and rigid boundaries is the main rule for therapists in any of these working environments, so that we don't take the patients issues home with us and they don't become emotionally attached to the therapist. Yet, I found that when I shared my journey through alcoholism and recovery with my patients, they felt they could trust me. They were able to open up and know that I knew what they were going through. This added a sense of calm to the sessions. The big question they ask is "How?" How do I get better? How do I get sober? Their faces would actually change as they realized that the person who is the therapist is saying, "Me, too, and this is how."

After a year at WPIC, I began my career as a full time therapist at Cranberry Psychological Center. I facilitate three main groups each week…Grief Club, Pleaser's Club and Family of Addicts Support Group called "From Chaos to Understanding". I feel I am most useful in this environment.

When I reflect on my earliest days in recovery, I could not have imagined my life as it is today. The "how" of it for me was that I kept coming back to the network of support I needed to continue into a life I knew very little about.

To have a book I can share with others was a faint hope in an all too familiar made up life in my head. When I met Hope Edelman, the author of *Motherless Daughters*, at an Association of Death Education Counselors convention in Baltimore and had a chance to discuss my plans on writing this book, she encouraged me to "Keep writing!" my story and assured me that I have something worthwhile to say. Yet, it was only when I took the actions myself that I was able to share this journey with others. The immeasurable fact to face is we can't change our lives for the better all by ourselves…we need help.

My hope is that you will reach out and find your own success story. Please – never, never, never give up. You can be okay!

{ ⋟ }

Appendix

Case Study #1

SUSAN WAS RAISED IN CHURCHILL, PENNSYLVANIA. BORN IN 1964, she was the youngest of three children of a family with their parent's marriage intact. Susan remembers her older brother, Johnny, was her protector, her guide, and her very best friend. Johnny, six years old when Susan was born, had been born with a cancerous tumor behind his left eye. Susan remembers her parents making multiple trips to New York City so that Johnny could receive the very best care possible.

Susan and their middle brother, Tommy, stayed at neighbor's homes while their parents and Johnny were in New York City for treatment. Susan confided, "Very little was ever said, when I was growing up, about what was happening to Johnny. All I knew back then was he was my best friend. I could tell he loved me very much, and I loved him more than anyone else in my life, all my life."

As a result of surgery for the tumor, he had an eye removed and replaced with a glass eye. "Johnny taught me how to ride a bike. I have never felt as loved and cared for by anyone as I did when Johnny was around." Susan remembered witnessing Johnny being teased by boys in the neighborhood and school. Susan said. "He didn't seem to be bothered by the teasing from the other kids. He had a great attitude about it. I always felt bad for him. I wanted to hurt those boys, who picked on him, but Johnny walked away from them and we'd walk home from the bus stop together. He never said a thing."

One day Johnny left and never came home. "Nothing was ever said. I knew not to ask about where Johnny was. He was gone. There was a funeral, and I wasn't allowed to go. I was sent to the neighbor's home. I've kept a stuffed elephant that Johnny brought back for me from one of his trips to New York City. That elephant remains a part of my most precious belongings."

When Susan came to me for therapy, she spoke about the accumulation of unresolved, unhealed grief. Her remaining brother, Tommy, drowned in a boating accident four years prior to her coming to see me. She stated that her family never, ever, talks about either of her brothers. Even now. "It is how grief is done in our family." Susan said. "Somehow if we don't talk about Johnny and, now Tommy, everything is supposed to be okay. I think about Johnny every day of my life. I drank a lot through the years but once Tommy died, my drinking took off without looking back. That is how I remember my parents solving most things as well."

From the age of six, Susan was overwhelmed with grief and the feeling of being alone. When no one informs children about anything that is happening around them, they feel lost and alone, as it was with Susan.   When experiencing grief, many people feel as though they are spinning out of control and out of their minds. Grief doesn't mean you are going crazy. It does mean you should reach out to others and get the support you need.

When families suffer grief and don't talk about the person they've lost, the silence and denial can eventually be deadly. Any other way of coping, besides seeking help and support, will ultimately bring more emotional pain and suffering.

Many cry "I feel so alone in all of this. I feel abandoned by my family who used to be able to help me through my pain, but now they are in their pain, too. I feel abandoned by God." It doesn't have to be this way. Let's start talking about it, all of it. With each feeling that we acknowledge and accept, we grow.

Case Study #2

One Sunday, not long after I moved to Wexford, I was reading a newspaper story which hit me like a ton of bricks. I often share this story with my clients, when appropriate.

The story was about a six-year-old girl who was in first grade. A nurse at her school saw bruises on her legs and reported it to CYS (Children and Youth Services). The little girl said she had fallen. Her mother reiterated the same story. Without any further investigation, this case was closed. In 1985, there were so many cases and so few people able to handle them that follow-up was non-existent.

The next year, when the little girl was seven and in second grade, her teacher noticed she had a large wound on her head and reported it to CYS. This time, the mother admitted she had beaten her daughter and the girl was placed with a foster family. There she found a loving environment with parents, two kids roughly her age and a dining room table at which to sit, be listened to, and understood.

It came to light that the girl's mother was a single mother with a history of rage and physical violence towards her daughter and many others. She was ordered to do an out-patient program of anger management (*which, by the way, makes the abuser MORE angry!*) After three months in the foster home, the little girl was taken in front of the judge and asked, "Who do you want to live with?" She, of course, said, "My mom."

The judge ruled that the little girl would go from this warm, loving, safe foster family back to what was familiar, her mother. For the next six months, the girl and her mother were regularly visited by CYS workers and the mother continued taking classes on anger management and parenting skills. It wasn't long before her school and CYS found out that the little girl had been taken to the emergency room with a broken leg and a head wound. Her mother had beaten her again.

The little girl returned to the foster family. They had normal routines for going to sleep, getting up and learning how to care for themselves in healthy ways. When the mother ended a nine-month rehab stint, the judge asked the little girl where she wanted to live. Again, she said, "With my mom." At this time, the little girl was eight and in the third grade.

Addicted to anger and violence, the mother had to have more, more often, and not long after returning home, the little girl was taken to the emergency with a severe head trauma.

Her foster family immediately took the little girl back and began proceedings to adopt her. The mother was placed in the county jail. Eventually, she was allowed to go back to her home and have infrequent supervised visits with her daughter. They met at a restaurant, supervised by either the foster family or CYS.

On the last visit, she was able to get her daughter alone, take her from the restaurant and back to their family home. She took the little girl to the basement and hung her. From state prison, the mother said that the girl told her she was sorry before she died.

This story is horrifying in its gravity and shock value. Most of us don't understand why the child would apologize to her mother. Psychology Today tells us that when a parent is abusive, small children often believe their behavior was worthy of the punishment they received. When children are young, they need security from a parent. If they don't feel safe, they can't learn self-worth. Without a sense of self-worth, children chronically feel insecure and will always blame themselves.

Any of us exposed to violence in our very young years can carry our child selves inside of us for the rest of our lives. Adults, who were abused children, will most often choose partners and friends who treat us the same way we have been treated in the past. So, that little child of long ago still remains a big part of the grown person as he or she chooses a mate.

The abuse cycle suggests that what was the honeymoon in the beginning of a relationship is what we look at and yearn for causing us to go back into a situation that is familiar, even if it is dangerous. We hope this time the person will be the nice person she or he was for a while in the beginning.

Even though clients with whom I share this story have immediate responses as to the extreme nature of the little girl's fate and swear nothing like that ever happened to them or anyone they know, given enough time, they are able to somehow relate. They often realize that they return to difficult situations or never leave abusive relationships because their discomfort is familiar.

{ 🕊 }

Photographs

*Grandpa Fabian and
Grandma Cecelia 1954*

*Gabriel
Mastroianni
1953*

*Josephine Zullo
Mastroianni 1965*

*Thomas and Mary
Zullo 1952*

*Clockwise from
youngest in front left
Leon, Ronnie, Bernie,
Noreen, Dad (Of
course!) 1941*

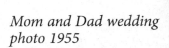

*Dad, Leon, Bernie,
Noreen and Ronnie
2014*

*Mom and Dad wedding
photo 1955*

Mom and Me

Dad and me

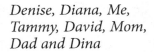

Denise, Me holding David and Diana

Denise, Diana, Me, Tammy, David, Mom, Dad and Dina

Chet and Katherine

*Luisa Roney with
Katherine 1992*

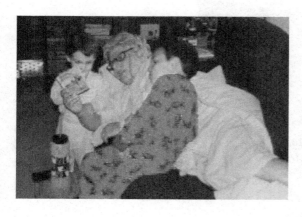

*Mom reading to Chet
and Katherine lying on
her right side on the left
side of the sofa 1993*

Chet and Katherine

Dad and Me, 2013

Mom and Dad a week before she died

{ ➤ }

Bibliography

Alcoholics Anonymous, Big Book. New York: Alcoholics Anonymous World Services, Inc., 1939.

Beattie, Melody. *Grief Club*. MN: Hazelden, 2006.

Brown, Brene. *Darling Greatly*. New York: Penguin Publishing Group, 2012.

Dubner, Stephen J. *Choosing My Religion*. New York: Avon Books, Inc, 1998.

Edelman, Hope. *Motherless Daughters*. Boston: Da Capo Press, 2006.

Erikson, Erik. *Childhood and Society*. New York: W.W. Norton & Company, 1950.

Huber, Cheri; Shiver, June. *There Is Nothing Wrong With You*. United States of America: Keep It Simple Books, 2001.

SPEAKING ENGAGEMENTS

Debra Whittam is available for speaking engagements.
For booking information, contact:
Turning Point International
(702) 896-2228

{ 🦅 }

About the Author

DEBRA WHITTAM IS A LICENSED, PRACTICING mental health therapist in Pittsburgh, Pennsylvania, who specializes in addiction, anxiety and depression, grief and loss. Whittam is passionate about her work in all areas of her specialties, especially addiction. Working in a detox unit for over three years before beginning her own private practice, Whittam realized, while counseling patients in the life and death arena of the detox unit, how much the loss of a beloved through death or a relationship impacted those struggling with addiction.

In this memoir, Whittam skillfully infuses her memories, stories and professional insights to remind us that the most important relationship we will ever have is with ourselves. She splits her time between Pittsburgh, Pennsylvania, the Adirondack Mountains in upstate New York and Paris, France. This is her first book.

CPSIA information can be obtained
at www.ICGtesting.com
Printed in the USA
FSOW04n2240280116
16269FS